STORIES, TALES

AND A

FEW SMALL LIES

OF A

COUNTRY PARSON

Ardella M. Curtis
209 Crow Canyon Dr.
Folsom, CA 95630-2086

STORIES, TALES

AND A

FEW SMALL LIES

OF A

COUNTRY PARSON

Robert B. Horine

Forward Movement Publications
CINCINNATI, OHIO

Cover design: Albonetti Design

© 2001

Forward Movement Publications

412 Sycamore Street
Cincinnati, Ohio 45202-4195
800-543-1813
513-721-6659
www.forwardmovement.org

Contents

PART I

ordinary times

Patrick and the Wolf

Patrick the cat scratches at my desk chair's back with his clawless front paws. I tell him it's still raining and he goes away for a minute, maybe two. Now he moves around to the side of the chair and paws my arm. If he gets no action this way, next time he will come lightly nipping at my sleeve.

We have played this game for about an hour. I am trying to edit a manuscript. Patrick wants to go out. Each time I open the front door he sees it's raining and goes back to the study. Either he has a short memory or he believes I can turn the rain off and on like I do the faucet when he drinks from it. Since this thought is perilously close to *hubris*, I settle for thinking Patrick is just impatient. I forcibly put him out the back door where he has some cover from the weather, and I go back to my work.

A few months ago I carried him in the same door. It was the night of the wolf.

Our young friend Becky, who now lives in Colorado, was back in Kentucky to visit her mother at Christmas. We invited her for dinner. Patrick and I were sitting in the living room when the doorbell rang. My wife—Becky the elder—and stepdaughter Molly, accompanied by Patrick, went to the door. I heard, "Is it all right if I bring my dog in?" Before I could say, "What about Patrick?" permission had been given and Becky the younger entered with her dog. The dog was not really a dog; he was a wolf. A friendly wolf, but still a wolf.

Patrick, who lives fairly peaceably with neighborhood dogs, knew a wolf when he saw one. He took the shortest route from the room—over the couch, across the end table (taking out a lamp and a potted plant)—finally launching himself from my shoulder. I have never seen an animal move so fast or with such purpose. He made one circuit of the house and, since no one had time to close the door, went out into the winter night.

During dinner the friendly wolf wandered about sniffing, drank a little from Patrick's bowl, and then settled next to my chair to watch me eat. "Is he always so friendly?" Becky the younger was asked. "Well, nearly always, unless he senses hostility or fear." I looked into his eyes and tried to send this message: "I am one with my brother the wolf. I am one . . ."

Through the evening we called for Patrick, and with flashlights searched everywhere we could. We tried to lure him by making the sounds of a cat food can being opened. I wondered if he would ever come home.

By 11 o'clock we had given up for the night and gone to bed. Patrick would be all right, wouldn't he? But the 11 o'clock news gave the wind chill as four degrees below zero and falling. No point in trying to sleep. I got up, went downstairs, and found the cat sitting on the back porch. When I opened the door he got the scent of the wolf and backed away. I caught him, wrestled him, said things I hoped would be comforting, and carried him inside.

For days Patrick lived upstairs where the wolf hadn't been. He lay by the hour on the landing, staring down the steps. If he slept, we never saw him do it. At last he went downstairs. But for weeks he moved cautiously, peering and testing the air, and he startled at all sudden movements and sounds.

Becky and the wolf are back in Colorado—if he hasn't eaten her—and Patrick now leads a normal cat life. He is selfish and he makes a nuisance of himself and some days

I wonder if he gives a twig for us. Nevertheless I am committed to looking after Patrick as much as he will allow—including searching on winter nights—and I am happy when, from time to time, he meets me on the front walk and rubs against my leg and comes with me into the house.

Lord, days and even years go by and we are satisfied that in the routine of our daily lives we are not only comfortable but secure; and then the wolf comes and we know better. We are grateful that despite our selfishness and our tendency to be a nuisance, that you care for us, that you are stronger than the predators that wait in the shadows, that you are willing to search for us in the cold and darkness of our terror, and that at last you will bring us into your house.

One Day When I Was a Kid

Aunt Louise ran downstairs crying, "The house is on fire!" I looked around for something to save. (Everybody was accounted for.) I grabbed my trumpet, headed out the door, and stood on the sidewalk listening to the sound of firetrucks coming from the Third Street station.

The fire didn't amount to much. A window curtain had caught fire from one of Uncle Clarence's creative wiring projects. My mother put it out with a bucket of water.

Family members ask why, of all things, I rescued the trumpet. At the time I had no answer. I treasured my comic book collection more. I was in the fifth or sixth grade and hated playing that horn. I had taken it up at the urging of Uncle Clarence, who was an enthusiastic cornetist, and kept at it for a number of years because I didn't want to disappoint him. So, I guess I saved the trumpet because of Uncle Clarence.

And Miss Elmquist.

One afternoon a week I left my school and took two buses across town to play with the all-city elementary school band, directed by Miss Elmquist. I loathed the two-bus trip across town, practicing late in the day, taking two buses home in the cold, damp darkness. My memory of those afternoons is like C.S. Lewis's portrayal of the bewitched land of Narnia; it was always winter but never Christmas.

I would have quit except for Uncle Clarence . . . and Miss Elmquist. She was tall and beautiful and from my seat in the shadows far back in the trumpet section I adored her. If only she would notice me. But she noticed only people like Ray Rector, the first chair trumpet, who could actually play.

If only she would notice me.

And then one day the all-city elementary school band was to give a concert on WLAP, our town's only radio station. Some wags said WLAP stands for We Let Anybody Play. Still, to play on the radio!

I don't remember all the pieces on the program. It was wartime and maybe they were all patriotic or military. I remember only "Anchors Aweigh." There we were in the big studio, playing on the radio. Our families were all listening. Maybe all 40,000 people in town were listening. We were something. Miss Elmquist was tall and beautiful and today she was also proud. She had brought us to the very pinnacle of performing art.

We played "Anchors Aweigh," and we were good. Maybe wonderful. Miss Elmquist was smiling. We came to the end where the words, if somebody had been singing, would say, "Here's wishing you a happy voyage home." I played the notes that went with those words. And then I played one more note after the rest of the band had stopped.

Miss Elmquist noticed me.

She never said anything. If only she had come to find me afterward and said, "Bob, it's ok. Most of your notes were good. Don't worry about it. I'll teach you how to play better." But she probably didn't know my name; it was a big band.

I carried on playing a couple of years into junior high school for Uncle Clarence's sake, but my heart wasn't in it. I didn't care whether Mr. Calloway noticed me or not.

To the people of Israel in the years before Christ, it

must have been like living always in winter with no Christmas—no Messiah, no great day, no good news. The people were waiting for God to notice them. They prayed, "How long, O Lord, how long?"

Why God took so long to act, I don't know, but finally he noticed the people (actually, he had noticed them all along). When he acted, he did something nobody expected, and few understood. He stepped down and walked back into the shadows among those who were unnoticed, and those who had played their lives badly, and he said, "It's okay, I'm with you, and I have some really good news for you. Don't worry anymore. Let not your hearts be troubled. I'm going to show you how to do this." And he did.

But there came a time for him to leave, to be seen on earth no more until the end of all things. As Christ prepared for departure, he tried to get his followers ready. It must have seemed to them that they were going back into the same shadows that he had lightened with his presence.

Jesus was foretelling the coming destruction of Jerusalem and its wonderful temple. He told them that there would be false leaders trying to sell them false teachings. He told them that the world was still going to have wars and natural disasters and hunger and sickness.

And if that were not enough, he told his followers that they would be arrested and persecuted, tried by courts, betrayed by family and friends, and even be killed. They would be hated by everyone because they were associated with him.

So, what was the good news? Despite all this, he said, you will not perish. "By your endurance you will gain your souls."

That's the way it turned out. They went through all that he had predicted. At first they were despairing, for the world did again seem so dark. Then, they discovered that the light Christ had brought into their world still shone. Now it shone within them, and shone from them and nothing could put it out.

Not many years later, one who believed in Jesus and believed the promise of imperishable life was able to write of the Christian experience: "We are treated as imposters, and yet are true; as unknown, and yet are well known; as dying, and see—we are alive; as punished, and yet not killed; as sorrowful, yet always rejoicing; as poor, yet making many rich; as having nothing, and yet possessing everything."

With St. Paul and all the saints we can join in the ancient psalm:

Shout with joy to the Lord . . .
Lift up your voice and sing.
Sing to the Lord with the harp . . .
[and even] with trumpets and
the sound of the horn . . .

Sentimental Journey

On a soft, warm day in late April I drove east into the Kentucky hills for a long overdue visit with old friends. We brought our stories up to date over meat loaf sandwiches at the Purple Cow Restaurant in Beattyville.

Rosemary and Mac Kilduff retired to her hometown after long service in federal government. Then they retired again after editing the local newspaper for several years. Mac was assistant press secretary for President Kennedy, who called him MacDuff. Mac was with the President in Dallas.

I hadn't seen the Kilduffs for some time. Around Christmas each year we vowed that not another year would go by without a visit. This time it was pretty much up to me. Rosemary, lovely as ever, is in pain much of the time. Mac appears healthy, but they both use oxygen part of every day.

Mac always has something new to tell. This time it was that when he was young he did some summer theater. As the cast of a new production sat around doing a read-through of the script, Mac said he had one of those experiences in which you look at a familiar word and it doesn't make sense. And so, "let bygones be bygones" was rendered by Mac—let's see if I can do this phonetically—"let b'go-nays be b'go-nays." The cast fell to the floor laughing.

Subsequent rehearsals went well. But when Mac said this line correctly on opening night, jitters and the memory of that first read-through caused the cast once again to go into hysterics, much to the puzzlement of the audience.

On the way to Beattyville I drove back roads by way of Clay City, Spout Spring, Hargett, the twin towns of Irvine and Ravenna, and Crystal, where what must have been America's smallest post office used to be located. The hillside trees' young leaves gave a backdrop of green haze to redbud and dogwood.

There had been storms the week before and many trees were down. The river road out of Ravenna was closed by high water and so I took the mountain road, stopping once while a highway crew cleared a tree from the right-of-way. Down on the far side of the mountain the Kentucky River covered valley farmland. A side road disappeared within a few yards into the brown water.

I was on my way to the Cathedral Domain, my diocese's camp and conference center ten miles west of Beattyville. I have made this trip countless times over more than thirty years, and I know the landmarks well. I miss the big old dog who lived for years by the river road and, whenever a car passed, chased his tail with such energy that in dry weather he sent up a cloud of dust.

A little more than two miles beyond Crystal I looked up; on a hilltop in the distance I could see the tall red cross of St. George at the west end of the great wooden cathedral. I drove up to the Domain to see a new dining hall and a new cottage. Both are far different than the rustic facilities I found on my first visit in the early sixties.

The interior of the old dining hall was being torn out. I spent some time there, reading the names hundreds of campers had painted on the walls. Nancy Stone, '71. She is now rector of a church in Florida. Meg. I'm pretty sure I know who she was. Many of these people were young campers when I acted as chaplain for some summer activities. Jeff Gibson, a friend of my daughter and her family. Somewhere—I didn't find it—is the spot where

Alex, Jeff's older brother, painted his name. He died a week later of encephalitis. The bell tower in the outdoor chapel is dedicated to him.

I copied this from the wall:

Walking alone I soon find myself lost
Walking with God I soon find my lost self
All of my time that I have spent searching
All of my time is spent in searching for God
No longer lost and no longer searching
I have found love in God to last my time

I asked the Domain manager, Andy Sigmon—a former camper himself—if he remembered Mark Smith, who signed the piece. Andy didn't. Neither did Dean David Webb, now retired and living at the Domain.

We now have a cathedral in our see city, but the Domain and the Cathedral Church of St. George remain the heart of the diocese. The first children who came here are long ago grown up, and they brought their children to the Domain and their children brought their children. It isn't just a place of childhood memories, or just a place where lasting friendships were made; it is a place of prayer, of worship, where generations have heard the stories of God's people, and have been in God's Presence. They have taken away from there what they have learned and what they have become and have given something of those treasures to their home parishes and to the communities where they live.

One generation shall praise your works to another and shall declare your power . . . They shall speak of the might of your wondrous acts and I will tell of your greatness. They shall publish the remembrance of your great goodness; they shall sing of your righteous deeds . . . They make known the glory of your kingdom and speak of your power; that the peoples may know of your power and the glorious splendor of your kingdom (from Psalm 145).

The name-bearing walls have been torn out by now.

I hope someone made photos. But if not, nothing of eternal value was lost.

When I left the old dining hall I walked down to the cathedral just, as I thought, as a small gesture of respect and remembrance. I was not prepared. A few steps into the building and I felt a rush as if I were reliving everything I had ever experienced there. It did not weigh me down, but rather lifted me up. It was wonderful. I stayed awhile.

Although I know that much of what I felt rose up from within me, I am certain that something came from the church itself, the palpable holiness of a building dedicated to God and long steeped in prayers and songs of thousands of campers and pilgrims.

I walked to the west window and looked down on the little garden cemetery of St. Mary Magdalene, where rest the remains of friends whose lives were deeply involved with the ministry of the Domain. And then I looked beyond Bishop's Point to the valley and the road by which I had come there. I hope to come many more times.

The Domain seems a God-haunted place. Certainly the souls of all who have dedicated our lives to God are so haunted. We and our Jewish ancestors have tended to think of God as a mountain God. We speak of mountain-top experiences. But Jesus told the woman at the well that in the future it would be more important to worship God in spirit and truth than to be concerned about where God was worshiped—mountain tops or even Jerusalem. "God is spirit; and those who worship him must worship in spirit and truth."

It was time to go down from the mountain.

I drove home by another way, passing Zoe and Shoemaker Ridge. I stopped at Slade at a rest area named in honor of Junior Williamson. He was not a politician. For years he came from his home in the mountains to the state capital whenever the legislature was in session.

He shined the shoes of the lawmakers, and they had a genuine affection for him. I suspect that from time to time his humble service reminded a representative or a senator that he or she, titles and honors aside, was a servant.

Spirit and truth, spirit and truth.

Babo and the Coal Pile

On a sweltering evening I came out of an auditorium on the campus of Transylvania University after being proud of my granddaughter's performance in a dance recital. Right by the exit the ground sloped away for 30 yards or so. This had been the only incline near my childhood home on which we could belly-flop with our sleds. We would take a run, throw our sleds and bodies at the snow-covered ground, and enjoy as much as five seconds of exhilaration. Then we would run back up and repeat until exhaustion sent us home.

We lived a half-block from Transylvania and the campus was the neighborhood playground. We also got some supplemental education there:

Basic economics: we collected tips for running errands for Air Corps cadets stationed on campus during World War II;

Spiritual development: On Sunday nights student pastors from the seminary gathered at a nearby restaurant to play pinball and brag about the day's collections;

History: Morrison College housed the tomb of Constantine Rafinesque and his ghost walked there;

Social skills: relaxing environment in which to philosophize and smoke.

The incident of Babo and the coal pile could come under spiritual development. It certainly was a religious experience.

Billo and Babo were brothers. They, the three Higgins brothers, my best friend Nolan and I played together.

We were 10, 11, 12—somewhere in there. We had no organized activities; our recreation was improvised. There was a huge coal pile next to our sledding hill at the back of the heating plant. Mostly we just climbed around on the coal. Maybe we threw some. The coal pile was shaped like a volcano. At the top you could look down in the center to a manhole through which coal was brought in to feed the huge furnace.

One day Babo climbed to the top, missed his footing, and slid out of sight. When his screams stopped, there was only the sound of a few chunks of rolling coal. Then nothing. Babo had fallen into the furnace. We were terrified. There was a lot of running about and yelling for help which finally brought us to the building's entrance just as the operator emerged looking surprised, with Babo—who was grimier than usual and crying, and I believe speaking in some foreign tongue. The hole in the coal pile led not to the furnace but to an inner storage area.

Babo cried for a while, then laughed and cried, then just laughed. Afterward we all laughed because our terror had turned into joy.

Remembering Babo falling into the hole sent me searching through what—with a straight face—I call "my files" for a short story I wrote years ago. Alas, I didn't find it, but I remember this much: It was about a man who, trying to hide out, changed names, clothes, modes of transportation, backtracked, and under the cover of darkness entered an abandoned house, went down deep in a hidden shaft, and in the darkness knew he had failed.

"Are you here?" "I'm here," said God.

Some holes we fall into, some we jump into with a will. How we get there makes no difference to God's presence or God's intention to turn our terror—or our grief or remorse—into joy, our crying into laughter.

Requiem
for the Saratoga

I admit I took a couple of bricks, but they were sort of obstructing the sidewalk—there on the other side of the wrecking crew's barrier. Well, three bricks: two for friends, one for me, from the walls of the Saratoga restaurant.

One brick was for Phil, a seminary classmate, now living in New Orleans. Another I gave to Anna. (She once went into the store next door to the Saratoga to buy a piano, but the proprietor refused to sell the one piano in stock. Puzzled, she left. Later I told her that though he appeared to be in the piano business, the owner was a professional gambler. Perhaps tired of refusing to sell the piano, he later went into the cactus business.)

Although the Saratoga had been closed for years, we gave up the building with a sigh. There was no question of saving it. Our city makes a big thing of preservation, but it's mostly talk before and weeping after the creation of another parking lot.

Most of the Saratoga's former clientele were from the neighborhood. Many have moved away or entered the Church Expectant. Newcomers go down the street to one of the ethnic, cute or theme restaurants. The Saratoga was none of those. It was just itself. In my days as a newspaper reporter covering city hall, I could find the mayor there most evenings, and if I hung around long enough he became talkative. Later, when I was in seminary, Phil and I took a meal there occasionally when we could afford it. We loved the place, and even the surly waitress whose table was often the only one available.

One night I told Phil a true story and he laughed so hard I thought he was going to fall out of the booth. Phil wrote the following during an Internet memorial service for the Saratoga:

"Sometimes that choice between the $2.95 and the $3.95 T-bone was maddening, especially when the utility bills piled high. I remember a . . . matron staggering to her feet at midnight of New Year's Eve . . . clobbering us all with the most exquisite, operatic rendering of "Auld Lang Syne" that my ears and heart have ever borne, and there was not one dry eye left in the Saratoga. After unrelenting standing ovations and . . . cries for encores, she sang it again and this time we all found our throats to join in, and "Lang" became our momentary deity, our epiphany in the heart of a dark and snowy night, our leap from death unto life . . . the Saratoga . . . served as the crucible of our priestly formation . . ."

Many of us don't take easily the passing of familiar places, as if they were containers for or guarantors of our memories. Sometimes we confuse the treasure chest with the treasure. Not long ago the church where my wife and I worship advanced a plan for the expansion of the buildings, better to serve the neighborhood and the community at large. One aspect of the plan called for moving the chapel stone by stone to a new location in the complex. In that chapel I had an encounter with God that changed my life radically. At first the idea of moving it gave me a twinge, but I got over it. Many did not, and though the plans have been altered to leave the chapel where it is, repercussions may cripple the whole project.

You know that it takes fifteen Episcopalians to change a light bulb—one to replace the bulb and fourteen to chant, "That's not the way we've always done it." Our legendary resistance to change has probably saved us from doing some very foolish things, but sometimes it has kept us from moving quickly when presented with opportunities to serve the Lord.

I had stopped going to the Saratoga long before it closed. It had changed; I had changed. My brick is still in the garage where I left it after its liberation. Maybe we'll make it part of the patio we plan. Every day it's more like a brick and less like an icon.

I used to have the idea that the older people got, the less able they were to handle change. The truth is that the inevitable changes that come with aging can help us to separate what's real and precious from what's ephermal and of little value in the context of eternity. I'm thankful for the Saratoga days and for the memory of them. I'm thankful the chapel was there when my life was in crisis, and gladder still that God found me there. But it could have happened on a street corner, as it did with John Wesley.

Thinking about a couple of bricks—well, three—has led me at last to revisit the final verses of Psalm 102:

In the beginning, O lord, you laid the foundations
of the earth,
And the heavens are the work of your hands;
They shall perish, but you will endure;
They all shall wear out like a garment;
as clothing you will change them,
and they shall be changed;
But you are always the same,
and your years will never end.
The children of your servants shall continue,
and their offspring shall stand fast in your sight.

Dog-Gone 'Coon

It may have been some sort of inadvertent perversity that brought this story to mind two days before the feast of St. Francis of Assisi. Do keep in mind as you read it that I don't squash a worrisome bug if I can find a way to catch it and set it free elsewhere.

On a winter night some years ago the Rev. John Madden and I sat late by the stove in his cabin by the Kentucky River telling tales. Somehow we got around to fox hunting and he told me about his grandfathers, who had lived on adjacent places in South Carolina. On Sunday mornings they would load up a truck with dogs, drive several miles, and turn them loose. Then the two men would go home, dress, and go to church. In church one would sit on each side of the nave, by a window, waiting and watching for the dogs to pursue a fox through the neighborhood. Because of the dogs' timing neither grandfather ever heard a sermon. Sunday afternoons were spent out with a truck rounding up the dogs.

There was also raccoon—'coon—hunting. That required another set of dogs. The dogs followed the trail of a raccoon and treed him, then kept him treed until the hunters arrived and dispatched him or, on occasion, let him go to be hunted another time.

There was one hunt that went badly. The dogs were well ahead of the hunters and caught scent of a 'coon. The chase took them to a pond and there they had their prey. Or, as it turned out, their prey had them. The 'coon was trapped, clinging to a log in the pond, and the dogs went in after him.

Now I didn't know this, and I must take John's word for it: raccoons are clever and strong and quite capable of handling a dog in water. They lock their arms around a dog's neck and hold him under. The 'coon has sense enough to hold his breath; the dog, not necessarily.

That day the hunters arrived at the pond to find the 'coon fighting for his life. Three dogs were dead. John's grandfather was armed only with a pistol—not the best weapon for hunting—and he was so excited and upset that he pulled his pistol, started blazing away, and in confusion shot two more dogs.

That afternoon was spent burying dogs. I don't know what happened to the 'coon. I hope he got away; I have a certain sympathy for the hunted. (John's parish is in the Bluegrass "hunt country" and once a year he blesses the hounds; I am, on the other hand, moved to pray for the foxes. Statistically, the foxes are in less jeopardy than the mounted hunters. Once the hounds did corner a pig, but it was rescued.)

It occurs to me that by the time John's grandfather arrived on the scene, it was a no-win situation for all involved. The poor dogs were overmatched by one raccoon, and if things weren't bad enough, their master arrived and caused more casualties with "friendly fire." The grandfather was obviously a loser. Even if the raccoon escaped, his day was ruined.

Maybe it was not St. Francis' Day that brought this story to mind. Maybe it was what I read every morning in my newspaper and see every evening on TV news. Maybe I think the dogs aren't nearly so stupid nor the raccoon so deadly as we are. We find ourselves immersed—drowning—in troubles we don't even know how we got into.

I thank God for the hope that there will come a day when "The wolf shall dwell with the lamb, and the leopard shall lie down with the kid, and the calf and the lion and his fatling together [and, we assume, the dog and the raccoon], and a little child shall lead them. The cow and the bear shall feed; their young shall lie down together; and the lion shall eat straw like the ox. The suckling child shall play over the hole of the asp, and the weaned child shall put his hand on the adder's den. They shall not hurt or destroy in all my holy mountain; for the earth shall be full of the knowledge of the Lord as the waters cover the sea" (Isaiah 11:6 ff.).

And not a minute too soon.

Dinner with
Harry and Sheila

When we arrived for dinner we found our hosts, Harry and Sheila Wagner, finishing up painting the kitchen. That was the first indicator that the evening would not go as planned.

Dr. Wagner was senior warden of our parish. I had just become rector and the bishop was to make his annual visit the next day. The Wagners had invited to dinner Warwick (Dub) Hale, the junior warden, and his wife, Darlene, my wife and me, and the bishop and his wife. Unfortunately, Harry and Sheila had not been able to move into their beautiful new suburban home until the day of the dinner. Things were a little hectic.

The kitchen was not yet in order and dinner was being prepared in the guesthouse, some distance from the main house. A cold rain was falling, and presently it began to freeze. Then the family's two horses got out. Horses are stupid about freezing rain and will stand out in it and catch pneumonia. In memory I carry a marvelous image of women in evening wear running about in the rain, waving their arms and whooping to drive the horses back into the shelter.

With the horses safe we awaited the arrival of the bishop and his wife. We waited and waited, six hungry people, including a couple who were by then pretty tired and stressed. The chief pastor of that far away diocese at that time was not consistently punctual and much time went by before someone—I think it was the junior warden—called the bishop's house. I should mention that the bishop, a fine pastor and teacher, was effective but not organized. Fortunately he had a small, efficient staff. Still, sometimes he outwitted their best efforts. He insisted on keeping two appointment calendars, and sometimes an appointment in one didn't get into the other. When Dub reached the bishop, he was at home, sitting by the fire, reading, having had his dinner.

The bishop joined us for dessert.

I called Harry not long ago to see if his memory of events matched mine. He said that he and Sheila had only a few days earlier recalled that evening. I suspect it has come to mind often over the years.

It seemed that everything was in place for a quiet, pleasant time. There were eight companionable people involved, the prospect of good food and conversation, the hours passing in a most pleasant, warm and comfortable house while outside the winter rain fell.

I can't help thinking that this parallels a continuing misconception of some of us some of the time about church. Good company, interesting discourse, inside with our love to keep us warm. But if the church life is not typically so discombobulated as that evening at the Wagners', things do go wrong. The physical plant will suffer a stroke, some people will not be where they ought to be or do what they ought to do, and inevitably there will be scenes at least as bizarre as ladies in evening wear trying to corral wild horses before they catch their death.

The church—parish or worldwide—is never quite as secure as we would like, and can't be, because both people within and people without, and the dynamics of relationships and the interplay of spiritual forces, are unpredictable.

The good news is that when we do our best to be God's people, horses get rounded up, eventually dinner is served, everybody makes it in time for dessert, and we do have our love to keep us warm.

Of course there is this footnote: it was not the last memorable gathering at the Wagners', gracious hosts that they were. Members of the parish men's group gathered at the Wagners' for a lobster feast. There were a lot of us present and the bishop also came. Lobsters were being dropped into boiling water and removed when ready and placed on plates. Different people were doing the dropping in and the taking out and it was in the hurry of this process that someone put a lobster in the pot and another took it out and placed it on the bishop's plate—where it crawled a little before being recaptured.

Less Zucchini, Please

Once a year in a large parish I served as rector, the Episcopal Church Women, with the help of husbands and other people, used to put on a dinner for patients from one of the city's Veterans' Administration hospitals. One day volunteers arrived in the afternoon to set up tables in the basement dining room and discovered that workmen building an addition had chosen that day to break holes in the outside wall.

There was a lot of scrambling, and dinner was moved upstairs to the chapter room. We were crowded and there was no air conditioning, but it was one of those times when you know Christ is present because you see him in the labors of the servers and in the faces of the served.

After I had waited tables for a while I sat with some patients and their attendants. A nurse, Jan, talked about her wonderfully productive vegetable garden and I listened with fascination because the only plant I ever had consistent luck with was a philodendron given to me as a birthday token in a former parish. It lived for ten years or so. I understand there's hardly anything you can do to kill one.

Jan said she had zucchini she would like to give away and I said I would take it along with any other vegetables she had a surplus of. It was the first offer of garden produce of the season and, while I'm not crazy about zucchini, I was willing to take it in order to encourage Jan to give me other garden produce. As it turned out I never got the other stuff. Only zucchini.

Why do people raise so much zucchini? It's not bad in zucchini boats and zucchini bread and zucchini cakes and mixed with other vegetables, but even when it's used in the most creative dishes, a person can handle only so much zucchini. And yet over the years it has been the vegetable most often offered to me. Sometimes bags of it have been quietly and anonymously left on my doorstep. I have been tempted to carry the bags quietly and anonymously to someone else's doorstep, but I fear discovery. What if I ignorantly left it at the home of the original donor? Although it would serve them right, it's just not done.

Why didn't Jan bring me tomatoes? Why don't all those other gardeners in my life bring me tomatoes? I've never had too many tomatoes.

I'm told zucchini is easy to grow and that's why there is so much of it. Maybe it's the philodendron of vegetables, hard to mess up, and so if you want to have a big successful garden you put in a lot of zucchini even if nobody wants it.

Next summer I hope to be offered some of the good things of the earth like corn and bib lettuce and figs. It's spiritually unhealthy to grow all that zucchini. But that's the kind of thing people do. We also grow guilt and remorse and grudges and judgments and such truck which don't take much cultivating and will grow season after season under the most adverse conditions.

Without waiting for next year, I'd like to have more forgiveness—for others and myself—and forbearance and compassion and care. Jesus said it was easy to do the things we oughtn't, and to travel the road to hell, and not so easy to do the right things and go the way of salvation. Fortunately, we have plenty of help. With God, all things are possible.

Next year, or even sooner, I'm hoping for less zucchini and more love.

Do Not Have Mercy!

As I write this in late January my thoughts have been occupied by forgiveness, a curse, and remembrance of a murder.

On January 25 we celebrated the Conversion of St. Paul. A man who had stood by approving of St. Stephen's death, who did we-don't-know-what to Christians in Jerusalem, and yet became the most powerful and effective evangelist in history. In intent Paul was a killer, but God claimed him, forgave him even before he asked forgiveness. (Paul later wrote "But God shows his love for us in that while we were yet sinners Christ died for us . . .").

That same week I edited meditations for *Forward Day by Day*. The writer is serving a life sentence for murder. That killer, forgiven by God, is another powerful and effective evangelist even in an Oklahoma prison.

The troubling event came with the 50th anniversary of the liberation of Auschwitz, where as many as one and a half million human beings, mostly Jews, were murdered. Most of us have seen pictures from the death camps. Some of us have visited the Holocaust memorials in Jerusalem or Washington.

The Nazis were not the only ones in history to slaughter people on a grand scale, but they were educated, citizens of a mid-twentieth century, civilized, Christian nation. This is the ultimate horror story, that someone who has been perceived to be respectable, good, turns out to be evil.

The anniversary reminded us of what Hitler and his followers did to six million or more people—Jews, homosexuals, Gypsies, the "mentally deficient."

Elie Wiesel, Nobel Peace Prize winner, was at Auschwitz for the ceremony of remembrance. He said, "I feel the fear and astonishment as I walk here 50 years later . . . You cannot imagine what it was like for them to arrive here at night and to see the immensity, the infinity of this place. Dogs barking, shots being fired, people falling to the ground, walking, walking."

Then Wiesel said this prayer: "Do not have mercy on those who created this place. Do not forgive those murderers of Jewish children here."

I didn't know what to do with that. I've heard a lot of people ask God to damn this thing or that person, but those words have been for so long almost casually used that seldom do we take them literally. This was different. Wiesel meant his prayer. How could this man, a man of peace, say such a thing to God? And for the world to hear?

As I struggled with this question, my mind went back several years. One afternoon after work I got on a parking garage elevator to find two of our employees, a mother and daughter, already there. I made a remark about a car almost hitting me as I crossed the street. The younger woman said, "I've got my Mace," and there in her hand was a can of the repellant. The driver of the car was her ex-boyfriend and he was stalking her. We got out of the elevator on the same floor. We left the garage driving in different directions. Less than five minutes later the stalker had blocked their car and killed them with a shotgun.

One of my co-workers, concerned about my reaction, asked the police chaplain to talk with me. I told him I hoped the murderer burned in hell.

Not exactly a prayer as we think of prayer, but real prayer is not necessarily what we say with our lips; it's what's in our hearts. On that day that was what was in my heart. I testified at the trial and the murderer is on death row. I have since prayed for him and I no longer hope he burns in hell.

Remembering, I understood a *little* better Elie Wiesel's prayer. It was what was in his heart. There is no use pretending about such things; God knows our prayers, even our unspoken ones. Better to get them out and let God deal with them and us.

To want hell for those who do great evil is a common first reaction. But willingly to hold onto that wish is dangerous to our souls.

The killer Paul and the killer in Oklahoma were claimed by God—reclaimed by God—and used to tell the Good News of Christ and in their lives to show his love.

The nature of the God we know in Jesus is a no-trade-in-needed love that offers forgiveness even before we ask it. We may pray for hell for our enemies, but we may not be confident of such a desire being fulfilled.

Two thoughts:

First, never-ending as God's love is, we must not presume on his forgiveness. It is possible to choose hell.

Second, we must not assume that those we judge evil and irredeemable really are. Paraphrasing C.S. Lewis: We may find in heaven that the worst monster we know has become a glorious, shining being that we are tempted to fall down and worship.

As God has mercy on the holy innocents in every age, may God also have mercy on those who hurt and kill. May God have mercy on us all.

God Here!

Yonder is the great and wide sea with its living things too many to number, creatures both small and great. There move the ships, and there is that Leviathan, which you have made for the sport of it.   Psalm 104:26-27

I have about given up hope of seeing a whale in the wild. My last try was an Alaska cruise. "Oh, you're sure to see whales," they said. One day the captain claimed he saw a spout off the starboard, but we all knew he lied.

The first time I set out to see whales, my son-in-law Chris and I boarded what was either a very big boat or a small ship at San Diego. Once we cleared the harbor the engine was shut down and we moved into the ocean under great sails. It was a wonderful experience and Chris and I went to the bow and stood searching the horizon for whales. We were also holding on. I had never been on a sailing ship and assumed this violent up and down motion was routine. Meantime, back in the cabins people were regretting their breakfasts. At last, even I became a little alarmed as the waves began breaking over the bow and soaking us. Now we really held on.

Presently it was announced that the ocean was not pacific enough and that instead of seeing whales we would be given a cruise around San Diego Harbor. It was not the same, but it was drier.

Seeing a whale at Sea World isn't the same as seeing one in the sea. Once in a German forest during a military exercise, I watched a fox go by very near my hiding place.

There was something about seeing him at home that touched my heart.

Someone gave me a recording of music that incorporated whale "song." About the same time I read Lewis Thomas's essay, "The Music of This Sphere" in which he says that underlying the signals one creature gives another—human beings and other animals—is a continual music. Some signals, he claims, have obvious purpose—a bit of birdsong that says "thrush here" or sounds in the ocean that say "whale here."

An extraterrestrial visitor might puzzle over his record collection, Dr. Thomas wrote. "The 14th Quartet might for him be a communication announcing 'Beethoven here,' answered after passage through an undersea of time and submerged currents of human thought, by another long signal a century later, 'Bartok here.'"

My wife Becky thinks Dr. Thomas's essay is on to something here, and that it explains the behavior of infants as we have observed it in church. For one thing, if an infant discovers another in a nearby pew, the child's attention becomes riveted on his or her contemporary, not on the sermon or any other adult presence or activity. The second thing is that in moments of silence in church we may hear a sound from a small person, say, in a back pew on the gospel side—"aa!" It is answered by an "aa!" from the epistle side near the chancel. Then a third baby gives this short signal from another part of the nave. Becky thinks the first one is asking, "Anybody there?" and what follows are answers. "Baby here." "And here."

Despite our incessant social organizing and our unceasing talk, talk, talk, there is in humanity a loneliness—the long loneliness—and there is an encoded signal in all of our communications to each other and it says "human being here" and longs for an answer. And like the babies, we do get answering cries and we receive them with joy and thanksgiving at a level far deeper than speech; "deep calls unto deep."

Through and under his words Jesus spoke to the people of the first century and "they heard him gladly" for he was responding to their yearning, and so he speaks to us now, and his answer to our cries is the best reply we could possibly receive—"human being here!" then "God here!"

Genevieve

On a gloomy evening during Christmas I passed a duck pond whose inhabitants seemed not at all bothered by the ice closing in around them. Why didn't they go south for the winter? And why do birds who do go south bother to come north again?

Anyway, I thought about Genevieve.

Genevieve was a white duck who lived on the reservoir—we called it Lake Moody after the Diocese of Lexington's former bishop—at the diocesan camp and conference center. She was, when we met, the only survivor of three ducks. A fox got the other two.

I was at the center for a men's Cursillo. Genevieve waddled up and down the road helping us welcome candidates. Occasionally she challenged a car, winning most of the confrontations, retreating only before the most determined drivers.

On Saturday morning Genevieve came up the road, climbed the hill to the outdoor chapel, and stood as if listening to the priest's meditation at Morning Prayer. Early Sunday when we were apparently making too much noise before dawn, she swam to the far end of the reservoir and quacked great obscenities. Genevieve was a character.

On my next visit to the center several months later the duck was still there, still the lone duck, and I felt something like compassion for her because she was alone. Do ducks care? Before I went to sleep that night I talked to God about a lonely duck.

The next morning, there on Lake Moody with Genevieve was a wild duck. Afterward I saw them together off and on for a while and then the visiting duck left. Going north, I guess; it was spring.

God didn't make ducks or people to be alone or lonely. That's why loneliness is so terrible; it's against our nature. But natural or not, there are an awful lot of lonely people.

God made us for each other, and like a mysteriously appearing wild duck he came to us in Jesus Christ to let us know that, no matter what, we would never really be alone. We Christians bear in us the life of Christ that can take away all the loneliness from the world . . . if we will. What a privilege, and what a job, and what a joy!

May we go into the world every day in the power of his Spirit, consciously and graciously offering our gift.

Love at the Green Lantern

I am back in a neighborhood where I lived a quarter of a century ago. Things change slowly here. Most of the small grocery stores and corner drugstores are gone, replaced by Kroger and Walgreens in the shopping center. But across the street Bob's Five and Ten, long established when I came to my first parish nearby, has outlasted Woolworth's.

Most of the restaurants I knew have gone, including the one where, as a newcomer, I was honored to address the local Kiwanis club—which turned out to be three fellow ministers in a back booth. I solemnly stood and said my piece and they solemnly gave me a certificate of appreciation.

Away from home, as I am three days a week, I have come tonight to the Green Lantern, the neighborhood tavern diagonally across 40th and Decoursey from Bob's Five and Ten. I am early and only three or four others are in the dining room, although the sounds from the bar room indicate the evening is in full swing there. Laughter and country music from the jukebox.

The Green Lantern is a venerable establishment. I had many lunches here when I was rector a block down at 39th Street, and several times parish dinners and parties were held in the dining room. Although I see no one I recognize tonight, the people here are familiar. And so is the menu. Lots of good American dishes, many of them fried. The last time I was here a month ago with my son and his family the special of the evening was an excellent meat loaf, but tonight it is tuna casserole. I can't believe it. Neither can Russell, seated with his wife across the aisle.

"Tuna casserole! God Almighty!" cries Russell in what I am sure is an earnest prayer. He mumbles in good humor to the young waitress. Then he calls toward the kitchen, "Is the cook Catholic?" Offstage, the cook answers affirmatively. Russell goes on, "You'd think they'd have something extra for us unbelievers." Actually, unbelievers are hard to come by around here. Variety of belief is plentiful.

Strangely, Russell orders and eats a bowl of cream of broccoli soup, then goes to visit Sue at another table. "How are you, Sue?" "Not too good tonight," she answers. "Well," Russell continues, "we all have nights like that. How many bypasses have you had?" Sue says four.

By 6:15 the tables have filled up with people who know each other and carry on conversations across the room. Russell tells a neighboring table, "This is a new waitress; you can treat her any way you want." I pay my check, wish the new waitress good luck, and leave.

Driving away I pass my old church. The lights are on as the rector prepares for the 7 o'clock Eucharist. Although many of the people who worshiped here 25 years ago have moved or died, quite a few "children" from that time are still faithful members, and the little church is more active than ever before in its 80-some-year history.

Episcopalians were a tiny minority in this neighborhood. Twenty-five percent of the people were Roman Catholic, a like percentage were of two kinds of Baptist, and the rest of us made up the other 50 percent— Episcopalians, Disciples, United Church of Christ, Methodists, Assembly of God and a dozen or so others.

We all got along well and intermarriages between Roman Catholics and Protestants created a small but steady supply of compromisers who became Episcopalians. The clergy met together regularly for lunch. We didn't talk much about doctrine, but just enjoyed each other's company. Those ministers and the parishioners I remember were like the customers at the Green Lantern tonight—people who like to eat and drink and talk and laugh together. And if we couldn't recite each other's creeds, there would have been few in the community who couldn't finish this sentence: "For God so loved the world . . ."

For God so loved Russell . . . For God so loved Sue . . . For God so loved the young waitress . . .

There is a kind of ecumenism that doesn't have much to do with the struggles of bishops and presbyters and deans and elders to hammer out some kind of scheme for church unity. It is an awareness of our human kinship that needs no concordat, but grows out of, and is nourished by, an understanding that "God so loved the world that he gave his only Son, so that everyone who believes in him may not perish but may have eternal life."

"For God so loved the world." All the people in it—the innocent and the fallen, the solemn and the funny, the Catholics and the Baptists, and the unbelievers—hoping they will believe. For God so loved you and me.

Despite the overexposure of John 3:16 at televised sporting events and as a quickly learned and easily remembered Bible verse for Sunday school recitations, it is still the most concise and understandable statement of the Good News of Jesus Christ, words that both plant a seed of faith and feed it as it grows. And when we go on to 3:17 we add comfort: "Indeed, God did not send the Son into the world to condemn the world, but in order that the world might be saved through him."

I'm glad to know John 3:17. If right now I could ask Russell, I think he would say the same.

Goodbye, Charlie Brown

"Rats," I said when I read the announcement that Charles Schulz was retiring and taking his "Peanuts" comic strip with him. "I'm doomed," I said, using Charlie Brown's favorite expression of despair. Where would I get new material for sermons?

In the weeks following the news of Schulz's retirement, several persons from parishes I have served said they had thought of me when they read the story. Since my ordination I have been delivering sermons by connecting biblical themes with episodes from the comic strip. Not every Sunday, but often enough that Charlie Brown and I became associated in the minds of parishioners.

The end of "Peanuts" gave a new meaning to the exclamation, "Good grief!" *Grief* in parting with the ageless little characters who had been part of our daily lives for about 40 years, and *good* in that we could smile and give thanks for the joy they had brought us.

Schulz gave us not only gentle humor but occasions to say to ourselves, "That's me! I know how that feels." There was one Sunday "Peanuts" that I especially remember.

Charlie Brown and Peppermint Patty are sitting, leaning against a tree. Patty says, "What do you think security is, Chuck?" Charlie answers, "Security? Security is sleeping in the back seat of the car. When you're a little kid and you've been somewhere with your mom and dad and it's night, and you're riding home in the car, you can sleep in the back seat. You don't have to worry about anything . . . Your mom and dad are in the front seat and they do all the worrying . . . They take care of everything."

Patty says, "That's real neat." Charlie Brown goes on, "But it doesn't last! Suddenly, you're grown up, and it can never be that way again! Suddenly, it's over and you'll never get to sleep in the back seat again! Never!" "Never?" asks Patty. "Absolutely never!" says Charlie. And Patty says, "Hold my hand, Chuck!!"

I know I used that in a sermon. And there were sermons that made use of Charlie Brown's unrequited love for the little red-haired girl, of Linus' telling the Christmas story, of St. Lucy the Crabby, of Linus' unflagging faith in the Great Pumpkin. Somewhere in a box in a closet are all those and many others. Someday I'll find them and read them over with a Snoopy-like whimper.

I did find one sermon, and I offer excerpts in personal thanksgiving for Schulz's long ministry which lovingly and with humor reminded us of our humanity: "There is a Peanuts comic strip that shows Charlie Brown sitting with Lucy, who is in her little booth with the sign that advertises 'Psychiatric help 5 cents . . . the doctor is in.' Charlie Brown, says, 'Sometimes I think I don't know anything about life . . . I need help . . . Tell me a great truth! Tell me something about living that will help me' . . . Lucy asks, 'Do you ever wake up at night and want a drink of water?' 'Sure,' says Charlie Brown, 'quite often.' Lucy continues: 'When you're getting a drink of water in the dark, always rinse out the glass because there might be a bug in it! Five cents please . . .'

"In the last panel, there is Charlie Brown musing, 'Great truths are even more simple than I thought they were.'

". . . Truth is as simple and straightforward as rinsing a glass in the dark because there might be a bug in it.

We're the complicators . . . we are suspicious of [truth's] simplicity."

I went on to say that there was one truth from which all other truths derive: God is Love.

The sermon continued from that point for several minutes—maybe too many. In a three-panel strip, Schulz could tell a great story. Remembering my "Peanuts" sermons, I marvel at the weight of words I sometimes laid on his simple presentations.

I'll miss Charlie Brown, Snoopy, Linus, Marcy, Patty, Pigpen, Spike, Sally, Schroeder, Rerun. And even Lucy.

Sigh!

The Methodists' Furnace

In her room at the nursing home, Elizabeth tells me stories about her hometown. She also gives me advice, such as, never fail to take up a collection when you hold a service.

A couple of stories are about her church. Elizabeth is a Methodist, but an Episcopal fellow traveler. One time, she says, her church had two notoriously bad singers and on a Sunday morning the minister announced that they would favor the congregation with a duet. Everyone groaned—inwardly, out of Christian charity—grasped their pews and began considering their minister's sanity. The organist played the intro, the two raised their songbooks, then turned them over to reveal the words, "April Fool."

My favorite story is about the furnace, and here, I confess, I may have done a little embroidery. But not much. On a Sunday morning the furnace was recalcitrant and during the service smoke was coming up through the heating vents. Ben, the sexton, could be heard kicking and cursing the furnace. At last the minister paused and asked a prominent member, Mr. Pitts, to do something to quiet Ben.

Pretty soon Mr. Pitts' voice was heard. "How are you, this morning, Ben?" Ben told him and colorfully described the furnace's high crimes and misdemeanors. Mr. Pitts then joined Ben in kicking and cursing the great iron monster. The minister stopped the service a second time and asked Mrs. Pitts to intervene. Presently there was a period of silence and the men, sheepish, returned upstairs. Then from the basement there was the sound of one more kick—a lady-like kick—and shortly Mrs. Pitts reappeared bearing a shoe with a broken heel and an expression of satisfaction.

Reflecting on Elizabeth's stories, I began to wonder whether Methodists have more fun than we do. Then I remembered a few things and put the thought out of my head. Serious as we are about the business of being Episcopalians, there are sufficient instances of quirkiness, if not downright hilarity, to put the Methodists in the shade.

In a parish I once served, a congregation of the deaf met on Sunday afternoons for a signed service. One Sunday the priest's young son was in the back of the nave making a terrible racket on the organ. Not wanting to stop the service, the priest piously turned toward the altar and in a great voice warned the boy of bodily harm unless the noise ceased. It did and the priest turned again toward the congregation and continued the Eucharist.

A predecessor in another of my parishes stopped a service when Mrs. Brown remembered she had left the burner on under her beans. When she had walked the two blocks home and back, worship took up where it had left off. The Browns also had a dog that attended all services.

One more: A couple of generations ago, a bird got into the nave of a large church in my hometown. Despite the best efforts of sexton and altar guild to shoo it out, the bird stayed, flying here and there, leaving unpleasant signs of its presence. At last the rector went next door to his uncle's home for help. The uncle came with his bird gun, and while he and his nephew were discussing the problem, he spotted the bird, fired from the hip, and brought the bird down with a single shot and no harm to plaster, wood, or glass.

Not much fun for the bird, but a notable event in the long and rich tradition of Anglican eccentricity. I will always remember Brother Bird when I pause for a moment in the parish garden beside the small fountain with the welcoming statue of St. Francis.

Singing on Galilee

Eighteen years ago, several months after I had begun to have serious problems with my voice, I was at the Sea of Galilee with a group of ministers. We stayed for a night or two in a kibbutz at the north end of the sea.

I didn't go there expecting miracles, but a couple of things happened that were at least remarkable. To me. To you they may seem quite ordinary. First, my voice was at that time not only whispery, but there were breaks in my speech. I'd be saying a sentence and there would come a gap; for an instant my vocal cords were completely paralyzed and then they would come feebly to life again.

I was feeling pretty low about my situation. I had been to a number of doctors, each of whom had a different diagnosis, all of them wrong. I had tried speech therapy, but the therapist said the problem was stress. Well, by then I surely was stressed, but that wasn't the problem.

One night we had a fire on the shore of Galilee and stood around it talking about what was on our minds, about hopes and fears. And with the little voice I had, I found myself saying, "I don't know what will happen, but I know God will have something for me to do."

Where that came from, I don't know. It certainly expressed more confidence than I had been feeling. That night a minister in the group found me and told me about a friend, also a minister, who had a similar problem and had been successfully treated. When I came home I talked with that man, and that led me to meet with another doctor who said he didn't know what was wrong with me but wanted to find out. The short version of the story is that I had treatments and even had a few months of remission in the mid-nineties.

But even leaving out the treatments, two remarkable things happened on Galilee. One was that I was my own prophet. God did have something for me to do and I would never have guessed what. The second thing was that when we left the kibbutz we went by motor boat some distance on Galilee to an ancient port, and on the way I stood in the back of the boat and began to sing *Benedictus es Domine*. I could sing. I couldn't speak very well, but I could sing. And I did, and it was, I'm sure, a coincidence, but rays of sunshine came through the day's overcast, and then a bird flew into the scene. If he had lit on my shoulder I would have died right there.

A great crowd of people had come to hear Jesus and they were hungry and he caused them to be fed. Then he sent the people and his disciples away and stayed for awhile to pray. The disciples were having trouble getting across Galilee. The topography causes sudden rough weather there. Jesus saw they were in difficulty, and late in the night—really between three and six in the morning—he came to them, walking on the sea, and he scared them. They thought they were seeing a ghost. And he said, "Don't be afraid, it's me." He got in the boat and the wind died. The disciples were astonished.

It's a good story, but some biblical scholars raise a question. Not for the sake of making trouble, for these scholars are devout people. The Greek words our Bibles translate "on the sea" can also mean "toward the sea" or "at the sea."

So, was it just a memorable event, or was it a miracle?

And let me go back to my night on the shore of Galilee. Was what I said and what followed just a string of happy accidents, or was something else going on?

I have my opinions. I think Jesus was walking on the water; otherwise, I can't think why Mark would have bothered to record the event. And I think what happened to me by Galilee and in the years following was more then fortuitous.

Jesus' presence when the disciples were struggling was a great relief; he brought calm and peace in a time of distress. And though at the end of their lives almost all the disciples were martyred, Jesus' continuing presence again and again brought them the peace that Paul describes as beyond our understanding.

I think I was touched on my visit to Galilee and at many other times since by that Presence that brings peace. And as you reflect on your own experiences I don't doubt you find that has been a theme—actually, *the* theme—of your lives.

Have you seen the movie, "The Perfect Storm?" Not every storm is calmed, and sometimes we go under, but if the Lord has joined us in the boat, it is enough.

St. Augustine, writing about this Gospel passage, said, "He came treading the waves; and so he puts all the swelling tumults of life under his feet. Christians— why be afraid?"

And William Barclay adds, "It is the simple fact of life, a fact which has been proved by countless thousands of men and women in every generation, that when Christ is there the storm becomes a calm, the tumult becomes a peace, what cannot be done is done, the unbearable becomes bearable, and [we] pass the breaking point and do not break. To walk with Christ will be for us the conquest of the story."

Not in the Script

In my former life as a newspaper reporter I was city hall reporter by day and entertainment columnist by night. The night work included movies, nightclubs, theater and, when need be, grand opera.

Since I spent most of my life at city hall I knew the mayor fairly well and liked him. But he drank more than was good for him, and perhaps because of this, often said what he actually thought. For instance, once when bids were being opened for station wagons for fire department battalion chiefs he listened to the cost and asked the city manager why the chiefs couldn't ride to fires in Volkswagens.

One night at a little theater performance by the Studio Players the mayor was in the front row. It was a time when the city was fighting the telephone company over a proposed rate increase and people were complaining about poor service. The play opened with an empty stage and a ringing telephone. Unfortunately, the phone gave only an uncertain and intermittent tinkling and the mayor said in a stage whisper, "Must be General Telephone." His comment was the highlight of the evening. Boring play.

On one occasion I was sitting in the front row. Maybe the mayor had inspired me, for I had an attack of whimsy. The play was "Blithe Spirit" and well into it there is a scene in which the actors talk about getting in touch with the Archbishop of Canterbury to exorcise some troublesome ghosts.

My fantasy was that I rise from my seat, step onto the stage, and announce that I am an exorcist sent by the Archbishop and that I understood they needed me. Can you imagine the wonderful confusion? What would they do—follow my lead, ad-libbing? Try to ignore me and go on with the play? Call for two large stagehands to show me out?

Looking back, I sometimes wish I had done it.

God has always done this kind of thing, breaking into people's lives, interrupting the action, messing up the script. The coming of Christ is the biggest interference, of course. During his few years on earth Jesus introduced himself into a lot of self-written dramas, saying a line or two here, adding a gesture there, inviting fishermen to follow him, visiting with scoundrels, healing a sick person, raising a dead one. And, what couldn't be tolerated because the script had not only been written but given the imprimatur, was his claiming to be a different kind of messiah and saying things about God being his father.

The people in Noel Coward's play didn't really want an exorcist; they were playing their parts. If an exorcist had stepped into the scene he would have been most unwelcome. It was much the same in first-century Palestine. The people, or at best their religious leaders, had already decided how God was going to act in history. The lines were written. Jesus' introduction of reality into the scene was unwelcome.

Maybe we shouldn't judge too harshly the people in that time. They had called on God for help for so long and they had waited so long that perhaps deep in their hearts they had stopped expecting God to do anything.

But God did and does.

We write our scripts and we include God's name at least for form's sake. We know what we want, what's good for us, what's good for family, church, country, and too often we set about to stage-manage and direct the whole production without taking God's presence seriously into consideration.

I think of so many people I've known—I'm among them—who have planned their lives and set out to live them only to have them interrupted by the Person who steps into the scene and says something, does something not in the script.

Catherine Miles Wallace wrote, "God blithely disregards the stories we tell ourselves about who we are. God steps in, with no sense of dramatic propriety, and God disrupts the probability and the verisimilitude of our own careful self-constructions. We think we know who we are and what we can do. Or at least we have invested a lot of care and a lot of energy in making reasonable sense of our own lives. But like that little beep on the phone line, God interrupts these conversations we have with ourselves" (in *Call Waiting*, an unpublished manuscript).

And we ought to be careful about casually writing God into our lives. God has no casual relationships. If we don't want him, it's probably better to be honest and up front about it. However, even that doesn't guarantee that in the middle of what we're doing a Stranger won't appear and say, "I believe you need me."

We do.

Yes, We Have No Pianos

Passing through our neighborhood shopping area on my way home from church, I noticed a vacant store building. It's a small building, a couple of times the size of an average living room. Several businesses have located there, but no one has made a go of it since Mr. Caruso.

Sometime back in the fifties Mr. Caruso opened "Caruso Pianos." In that small space there was only one piano on display. It was a baby grand, a beautiful instrument. I saw it often as I walked past—very often and for a long time.

One day a friend, a university professor, decided she wanted a piano and so stopped in at Mr. Caruso's. She walked around the piano admiring the workmanship, and then she sat down and tried a few chords. Only then did Mr. Caruso come from the back room.

My friend told the proprietor she liked the piano and wanted to know the price. Mr. Caruso discouraged her from buying the instrument. The professor said this was what she wanted. Mr. Caruso suggested that Templeman's downtown had a much better selection and that she should look for a piano there. My friend has a strong will and the conversation about this particular piano went on for some time. Mr. Caruso held out longer, and his would-be customer went away puzzled.

Puzzled until she told me about the experience. You see, I had been a newspaper reporter in my earlier life and I knew something about Mr. Caruso and Caruso

Pianos that the professor didn't. The piano business was what is called in grade-B gangster movies a "front." Mr. Caruso was a professional gambler. He didn't want to sell his piano; if he did he would have to go to the bother of getting another one.

It may have been that the stubborn professor was too much for him. Or perhaps there was beginning to be too great an interest in his piano by numbers of people. Anyway, soon after that Mr. Caruso quit the piano business and began to display cactuses.

I don't remember how long that establishment lasted. Mr. Caruso died a few years ago and no one has been successful in the store building since.

As I remember Mr. Caruso, the professor and the piano, a couple of thoughts occur to me. The first is that we shouldn't display things unless we're serious about offering them. We shouldn't pretend that we care if we don't. It will at least be embarrassing and maybe hurt somebody if we're called upon to deliver and don't do it.

The second thing is kin to the first. It is that most of us have something in our lives—something or maybe even a personal relationship—like Mr. Caruso's piano. We live what we consider a good life, we behave acceptably in society, but we have one thing that we would consider too dear to us to let it go no matter what. And the truth is that is just exactly the one thing that Jesus tells us we have to give up. (Remember the rich young man who kept the law but wouldn't give up his money to follow Jesus?)

Being a Christian is a strange sort of life. We may try out several approaches to living, like all those businesses that came and went in the little store building. Some may seem to be doing okay for a long time, like Mr. Caruso's pianos and cactuses. In the end, though, it's not what's in the show window that's important, but what's going on in the back room.

Blessing, Next Right

My last parish had many young families who were forever moving and I blessed a lot of houses. Toward the end of my tenure Lexington was spilling over into the next county and my movers who wanted the country life had to move further and further out.

A couple of out-of-county houses were off main highways and then off secondary roads and pretty much at the end of tertiary ones. Directions to these places were given like treasure maps: turn left at the old oak stump, go three-tenths of a mile until you come to a red, white, and blue mailbox, then wait for the sun to set between the two hills; the last ray of daylight will fall on a three-legged goat who will point with his remaining forefoot toward a cabin whose occupant will give you a riddle that will lead you to your destination.

Terry and Kathy Jo Gutgsell and their children moved to the country. Their directions were simple, but given in tenths of miles. I've never trusted an odometer and was a little nervous about finding the right house. As we drove along saying "There's one tenth," etc., and trying to guess where our calculations would bring us, we saw posted at the entrance to a driveway a sign which said BLESS-ING and pointed the way.

That happens a lot in my life. I get to fretting about this or that, or feeling frustrated in trying to save the world, wondering how things are going to come out, and suddenly I top a rise and there's one of God's signs— BLESSING—with an arrow.

Sometimes it's a note of thanks or love that comes unexpectedly with the day's mail. Maybe a phone call or a friend stopping for a minute. Maybe a passage in a book that says something I need to know. Maybe a time in prayer when God's presence is felt intensely. Or—and this one is the hardest to explain—blessing in the pain or anguish of a troublesome, even threatening situation. When Jesus gave the beatitudes, what he said, according to Luke, seems to point to future reward for troubles now; but a close reading hints of the mystery of blessing within the troubles.

One of our most common spiritual problems is looking only for relief from something, looking only for a way out, instead of allowing God to be known in whatever it is that's bothering us.

Bless a house? What does it mean to bless something? We have priests who bless automobiles and boats and pets. The manual I have in my study has scores of blessings listed from "Advent Wreath" to "Wreath, Advent," and in between are such things as ashes, banners, bridges, children, first fruits, crops, lambs, nets, pregnant women, ships, spacecraft, throats and windows, and just in case something was left out, there's a blessing for "Anything Whatsoever," with appropriate blanks.

A blessing is a gift from God, a little something to give us happiness. Like other gifts, some of the best are surprises. Some make us laugh and some make us thoughtful and some bring tears. All bring the giver—God—and the receiver—us—into a special moment, maybe just the merest part of a second, when we know who God is and who we are and we enter into joy.

The assurance we have is that, wherever we are, God is there too, that the Kingdom of which we are citizens is not a place with borders and customs officials, but a homeland that exists within its citizens.

The Kingdom of God is not so much like a place we're on our way to and where we'll arrive on a particular day and set up housekeeping, as it's like a trip in a car with the family on which we stop along the way to visit here and there, stop for picnics, suffer flat tires, fusses, car sickness, icy roads and confusion, play games, sing songs—a trip for which we have some directions (often misread) but in any event on which we have more fun going together than alone.

Priests give the authoritative pronouncement of God's favor. But we're not the only ones who give blessing. We all either give it to—or withhold it from—each other. By our treatment of each other we give assurance of God's favor or we say, by indifference or neglect, that God—at least through us—isn't giving anything.

That's a lie. God is trying to give us and everybody we meet his favor, his life, himself. The only thing that gets in the way is us. If we center on ourselves, we tell that lie, we block the blessings that God intends for us and for our brothers and sisters.

Despite our economic problems, we Americans still live in a pretty affluent society. But even among those of us who don't have to worry about food and shelter, who have enough income to pay for amusement, diversion—even among us there is much unhappiness. Maybe a lot of it is because of our mobility, or rootlessness, a constant motion that allows us to have acquaintances in many places, but makes it difficult to know people, to make and keep friendships, to know uncles and aunts and cousins.

There is unhappiness among us, among these people that God loves, and I think that even in our mobile society we can do something about that for each other. We can give blessing, we can be blessing, and if the time we have with each other isn't as much as it used to be, as much as it might be, we can still give and receive happiness.

Maybe that's the mission of today's congregations of

mobile Americans—to come together for a little while to bless each other before we go out again into the world. Maybe a little while is enough. I suppose it's all a matter of degree; everybody is just passing through, and some stay longer than others in this life, but not by much.

If impermanence is bothering you, remember that one of our most common spiritual errors is looking only for relief from something, looking only for a way out, instead of allowing God to be known to us in whatever it is that's bothering us. The Gutgsells didn't move back to Lexington for my convenience, but they did put up a sign so that in that strange land of Jessamine County we could find friends, shelter, could be in a place where there was blessing.

It's a wonder and a joy of being a Christian that we have the certainty that, no matter what alien land lies over the next rise, there will also be a sign that says BLESSING, with an arrow.

Me? I Believe in Love

Sometime last year I met an old friend for lunch. We had long ago both been disciples of the late Bishop Addison Hosea of Lexington. Whenever we got together over the years, we always talked about him—talked about what a wonderful teacher and pastor he had been, laughed about some of his eccentricities, his less than organized work habits. Wondered whether we did the right thing in taking this good priest and making him a bishop. Too late now.

My friend is a scholar, an intellectual, forever examining and re-examining his beliefs. The day we had lunch came in the midst of a time when he was struggling with his faith, with the meaning of life, the nature of God and humankind. And my friend was questioning where he, himself, fit into the great tapestry of reality.

Mostly, I listened. At last he said to me, "What do you believe in?" Now, you may think computers are fast, but they are nothing to the human mind—even my own. In an amount of time that you can hardly call an amount, I examined and discarded all possible answers to that question but one. For instance, my friend is quite knowledgeable about theology; I suspect he knows a good deal more than I do. It would do no good for me to recite a creed or to quote scripture or cite a scholar.

"What do you believe in?" and I said, "Love. I believe in love." He sat back in his chair and it was as if he had drawn a great sighing breath of the spirit. He knew exactly what I meant, and it was, I think, the only possible right answer to his question on that day.

Neither of us knew it, but my friend was about to face a great trial in his life, and I have thanked God for the question and the answer. I believe it helped prepare him.

The experience also changed me. It changed even the way I see things.

For instance, on the routes I take for my morning walks, there are five churches. Always I have seen them just as five churches—Greek, Roman, Lutheran, Baptist—and a nondenominational church whose name I can never remember. But on a morning after that lunch I saw them as something more. Each one of them is a symbol, a big symbol, a tangible symbol of love, that great love that pervades people in all places at all times, times past and times to come—love that burst forth two millennia ago like the big bang across and through all dimensions of reality.

Every one of those churches was built by people who recognized that God is love. They began the journey of faith, as had Abraham, without knowing where they were going, simply trusting that they would end up where they belonged. On the way they built churches—signs of God's love, places to shelter for awhile, but not places to stay—places from which to go on, and on.

Freud said that religion is the universal attempt to recapture the contentment of the womb. He got it wrong. Like Father Abraham we go in faith from what seems secure, outward through uncertainty, and find deep blessing. Being a Christian is, someone wrote, the peace that is no peace—a willingness to go, without any guarantees, without maps, when God says go—and to begin again.

Too Many Syllables*

I work in Cincinnati, and on fine spring or fall days—summer is too hot—I carry my lunch bag to Fountain Square. The air seems cleaned by the fountain; there are exhibits and shows, hawkers, pigeons, characters and pretty girls. As often as not there's a preacher.

One day as I finished my hot dog and started on my Coke, an old man approached and sat down beside me on the wall. He was short, white-haired, ruddy of face, wearing khaki trousers with suspenders, and a faded blue shirt. He was also sucking on a corncob pipe and I had noticed him because he reminded me of my grandfather. Maybe he came over because I was looking, or maybe it was my clerical collar.

"Listen to that fool," he said, indicating with the stem of his pipe the preacher of the day. "Tellin' people Jesus is comin' soon to send 'em all to hell. Notice how many people are stoppin' to listen. (*None*) Funny kind of gospel, ain't it?"

I agreed it didn't sound much like it. His accent told me he had come to Cincinnati from the Kentucky hills. We might actually be kin.

"You a Cath'lic?"

"No, I'm an Episcopalian."

"We had one of those churches back home. Didn't amount to much. I mean they didn't have many people. Mostly mine owners and bankers, some teachers; a doctor, I think. No, not a doctor, a dentist. Called him

---

*A work of fiction

doctor, though. Everybody just thought they were somethin' like Cath'lic, except the priest was married and didn't wear black all the time.

"Now, me, I knew better. I had a cousin moved to Lexington and went to the university and joined the Episcopal Church. He told me all about it, how it was really protestant and catholic all at once."

He took time to refill his pipe with Prince Albert, light it, tamp it with the end of a charred finger, and light it again. Then he went on:

"My cousin died last year. We went down to the funeral. I will say, I never saw one like it. It was grand. You'd think a church with services like that would pack 'em in. We stayed over in town till Sunday and went back to that church and the service that morning was somethin'; it was beautiful. My wife still talks about it."

"Well, maybe that's the secret," I said. "If we could just get people to *see* an Episcopal service, we could hook them. As it is, we've been losing members for the last twenty years."

"Yeah, I know," the old man said. "My cousin said it was all the hoo-rah over havin' women preachers and changin' your Prayer Book. But you know, I studied about that and I told him—before he died, this was—I said, 'Tom, that ain't the trouble with your church. The trouble is with what you call it, the name of it.'"

He turned to me and began to speak earnestly, making his points with his pipe stem.

"Episcopal! Where in the world did you get a name like that? It's worse than 'Presbyterian!' Nobody can hardly pronounce it unless they practice sayin' it for a day or two. And another thing, words remind people of things and make 'em feel certain ways. Episcopal makes me think of an Adam's apple; I reckon it's because the *cop* causes me to use mine. Anyway, it don't make people think of anything pleasant or upliftin'. It sounds kind of snobbish, or maybe foreign.

"And it's not easy to spell. I'm not just talkin' about uneducated people, but in that last twenty years you're talkin' about, people have been listenin' and watchin' TV, not readin' and spellin'. Everybody's kind of lazy, mostly, and if it comes to havin' to spell Episcopal or Baptist, for instance, they're gonna take a two-syllable church like Baptist or Cath'lic every time. Besides, those names conjure up images. Episcopal don't connect with anything.

"Back home, when somebody died and they weren't sure what religion they were, they usually put Baptist or maybe Christian in the obituary. Never did six syllables like Episcopalian. That's one reason there are so many Baptists and Christians and Cath'lics across the river in Kentucky. Or anywhere else, for that matter. Why, even Luther'n you can get into two syllables if you hurry.

"You listen to me, son. You all do a wonderful worship service, but people are driftin' away and new ones ain't comin' because they don't find the name attractive and they don't want to fool with it. People have a yearnin' in their heart, and Episcopal don't call to it.

"You get a nice, smooth, short name, and you won't have enough pews for everybody. Somethin' like the Church of Beulah, or one with words like heaven or home or Jordan or Jesus—something short and good and holy sounding, a name that says something. Next thing you know, you'll be up there with the Baptists and the Cath'lics.

"I might even come back myself," he said, knocking out his pipe into his hand. He walked away and stood watching the haranguing preacher for a moment, shook his head, waved at me without turning, and went off through the arcade toward Sixth Street.

Glum in the Balcony

This story may not be the absolute, literal, inerrent truth, but it is, nevertheless, truth—if you get the distinction. Memory is imperfect.

My high school, Henry Clay, in Lexington, Kentucky, had an annual student night with a prize for the best act. One year Bill McCauley, Syl Kiger, Allen Douglas and I got together to create a sure winner. It would be spectacular, even stupendous.

There would be music, comedy, people swinging in on ropes. We started planning weeks in advance. We planned and planned and discussed and debated how this or that was to be done or whether it should be done at all or something else altogether. We talked so long that on student night we were sitting in the balcony watching the show when Howard Parks came on stage in a white sport coat, stepped into a blue spot, and to piano accompaniment sang "Blue Velvet," a simple love song of the day. Not only did Howard win the prize, but he "moved" a number of girls and won the envy of many boys, including four big-time showmen sitting glumly in the balcony.

(You probably see already where this is going, so I will digress long enough to tell you that one afternoon as Howard and I passed the Air Force recruiting station, I somehow talked him into going in and signing up. He reminded me of this when I saw him at a high school reunion 25 years later. I am now a little uneasy about my motives that afternoon. Patriotism or revenge? Oh, well!

As Kurt Vonnegut says, "So it goes.")

Bill, Allen, Syl and I were so busy talking about details and complexities, with getting our version of the act approved as the "right" version, that nothing got done. Howard sang a simple love song and got people's attention.

I am of the opinion that Episcopalians talk too much about what ought to be done and how to do it, and act too little, and that the "better" organized we are, the less productive we become.

I am thinking of Jesus' command to go into the world and make disciples. I am thinking of the Decade of Evangelism and wondering if we are so distracted that we have forgotten how, or lost our ability to sing a love song, to make a simple proclamation of the coming of the Kingdom of God.

One of the wonderful things about our church is our concern for justice, our compassion for the poor and the oppressed. And so we are always busy, busy, busy debating issues of one kind or another—what should we do, how should we do it, who gets the money, who gets our attention. And we debate theological and moral issues—is it this way or that?

Important issues must be addressed, but our talk too often distracts us from paying due attention to those outside the church who are hungering for the Good News that God loves them, that God wants them to live with him forever and that God has made a way for that to happen. Our endless talk is also confusing for many people in our parishes and missions, those who do not sit in the councils of leadership.

Another danger is that our important issues, which are issues of love, become issues of authority, and issues of authority become issues of power.

One lesson we may have learned in Phoenix at a General Convention. Although church government is set up on a democratic model, the church is not just a democracy. We cannot resolve issues by majority rule. Unless what is passed is in our hearts, legislation is at best a fruitless exercise, and at worst an act that more deeply divides us.

How the Devil must laugh when we are paralyzed by disagreements over who is the rightest, who is the lovingest, who is the holiest. Our church doesn't need more talking; we need more listening—to God and to each other. We need to listen and learn God's love song and then sing it.

I am impatient with our endless talk when I remember a letter I received last spring from a Sudanese bishop living in exile in Kenya. He didn't even know, in the midst of his country's civil war, where his family was, or whether they were alive. But he was about to go back into the Sudan to find them and to serve his people. I may not hear from him again. And I remember words from Chinese Christians who went on worshiping and evangelizing in secret under a repressive government. They wrote, "Not until the flags of love are planted all over the world should we think that we have done our duty."

Perhaps it would help our vision if for the rest of this decade we called ourselves by our official corporate name—The Domestic and Foreign Missionary Society of the Episcopal Church in the United Sates of America.

Some people blame the news media for our some-times absurd image. But the news people aren't in the Gospel business. I know; I was for years one of them. They aim at making money, and they make it by report-ing surprises, fights, scandal, tragedy, demagoguery and buffoonery.

If we are frustrated by our inertia, what are we to do, we who have little power or authority? Maybe the little people of the American Church should form a new religious order. We might call it the Friends of Jesus. "Friends" Jesus called those who chose to obey him. Our standard might be the confession, "Jesus is Lord." And we might have just two rules. The first rule would be this: Before all else . . . to give bread to hungry hearts and water to thirsty spirits. The second rule would be that there aren't any other rules.

But to go back to the original metaphor, inspired by Howard Parks and the love song. First we listen, because we can't give away something we don't have. We listen to God's love song, listen carefully, listen every day, listen in quiet so we can hear it clearly. And then, in what we do, in every act, be it the small kindness of a smile or putting our lives on the line—in what we do and especially in what we are—as individuals, as families, as congregations—we sing the love song. We sing it even when it seems lost among the persistent voices of those who equate power with righteousness and loudness with prophecy.

Did you see the movie *Field of Dreams*, or read Kinsella's book *Shoeless Joe*? An Iowa farmer hears a voice saying that if he turns a cornfield into a baseball field, Shoeless Joe will come. The voice says, "If you do it, he will come."

If we sing the love song, they will come—those whose hearts have no home, whose lives are without love, who do not know joy, whose way is uncertain, those whom no one has comforted, those who have fallen and no one has lifted up. They will hear God's love song and they will know that we have been with him and they will come.

The Pelican Legend

In a couple of months I'll be at a beach in North Carolina sitting in the shade, enjoying the ocean breeze, just being.

Oh yes . . . and watching the pelicans. Great squadrons of them fly west in the morning and east in the evening, and now and then one or two will break off and dive into the surf for a morsel. Pelicans use that great pouch (that makes them look as if they have a thyroid condition) and their bills to scoop small fish. They don't, as some people think, store food in there. They swallow what they scoop.

I love pelicans.

Interesting bird. They live in colonies and often help each other fish. They swim together in a line, beating the water with their wings, driving fish before them, then scooping them up in their bills.

The young ones feed by putting their heads deep into the mother's pouch to retrieve partially digested food.

Which brings me to the most fascinating thing about pelicans, the legend that when there is no food to be had, the mother tears her breast and feeds her young with her own blood.

Whatever the origin or the truth of this tradition, it has made the pelican a symbol of charity, of mother-love, of self-sacrifice, sacred especially to Christians.

The Holy Land is filled with places where this or that event or miracle happened—"traditionally." Who knows? Is this place on Mt. Tabor the spot where the transfiguration took place? Does this footprint in the stone on Mt. Scopos mark the site of Christ's ascension? Is this really *the* stable? Was the crucifixion and burial here or there?

There are some places known to be authentic. The synagogue at Capernaum. Jesus taught there. Gethsemane. Jesus prayed and sweat blood there. The Wailing Wall. Jesus knew that wall as part of the Temple.

In other places there are tantalizing clues. There is in Jerusalem an upper room which tradition says is the site of the Last Supper. It is unimpressive until the guide shows you a little column by a stairway. The column is from the first century, near the time of Jesus' physical presence. At the top of the column is a carving. Pelicans, feeding their young from their own bodies.

"I am the living bread that came down from heaven," Jesus said. "If anyone eats this bread he will live forever. The bread that I will give him is my flesh, which I give so that the world may live . . ."

"If you do not eat the flesh of the Son of Man and drink his blood, you will not have life in yourselves. Whoever eats my flesh and drinks my blood has eternal life, and I will raise him to life on the last day . . ."

Jesus said this as he taught in the synagogue in Capernaum. Some of the people who heard these words had real trouble with them, because their use of language was basically literal in expression and understanding. Many of Jesus' disciples left him after they heard this.

But we understand: "This is my body . . . this is my blood . . . All of you, take them: I will be with you whenever you do."

Jesus gave himself—gives himself—his flesh and blood because the world is starving. We understand that.

He said some other things, too, and they're hard for some of his present-day disciples to take: "As you sent me into the world, I have sent them into the world . . ." What a mission, to be sent into the world as Jesus was!

In response we say in the Eucharist, "We offer and present unto thee, O Lord, our selves, our souls and bodies, to be a reasonable, holy, and living sacrifice unto thee . . ."

Just saying those words isn't hard. It doesn't hurt, and we can go away with ourselves intact, feeling a little better than when we came into church. But to say the words and mean them: how much does that cost? How much of ourselves must we put into that offering?

It's easy to feed someone out of what I have if I have a lot of it. It's easy to give away what I don't need. But what happens when there's nothing left except ourselves, when all I have to give is some of me and my life? What happens then?

Can we tear our breasts and give our selves, our souls and bodies, our life's blood, our spirit? Can we give *our selves*?

The answer is, yes, we can. "Love each other as I have loved you," Jesus said. We can do that *because* he has loved us. Because he gives himself, and because we come near him to receive him, to take his flesh and his blood, we can take his life, too, his Spirit, and we can do good things, loving things, even heroic things because we don't do it alone.

Are we sinners? Cowards? Failures? Hypocrites? Lazy lay-abouts? Timid? Doubters? Maybe, sometimes, but we're also the people Jesus loves and gives his life to, and pitiful, self-serving specimens we may be, but in trying to obey the Lord we are his friends and the children, the young, of God, and he feeds us of himself and in the strength of that gift we survive and confound our enemies and amaze the world and ourselves.

"Whoever believes in me will do what I do—yes, he will do even greater things, because I am going to the Father. And I will do whatever you ask for in my name, so that the Father's glory will be shown through the Son. If you ask me for anything in my name, I will do it."

The Last Truth

In Beattyville, Kentucky, not only do people know everybody else, but they know their dogs, too. My friends Malcom (Mac) and Rosemary Kilduff live in Beattyville. They're both retired from federal government jobs and now retired a second time from writing and editing the local newspaper. Rosemary is a sweet lady and Mac, although he sometimes pretends to be a curmudgeon, is really a great-hearted, humorous man. This is one of his stories.

People in Beattyville *do* know everybody and their dogs. One day Mac and Rosemary were down on Main Street when they spied Wooly, a little dog belonging to Greeny and Carol Kincaid, hanging around in front of the Purple Cow, Beattyville's premiere restaurant. The Kilduffs, thinking Wooly was too far from home for her own good, coaxed her into their car and drove back up to the Kincaids' house. No one was home so they took Wooly to their house, told her to stay on the porch, and went inside. She happily stayed.

Later, Mac called Greeny and told him he had Wooly safe at his house.

"You've got who?"

"We have Wooly here on the porch. We found her downtown and were afraid she'd get hurt."

"No," said Greeny. "Wooly's right here with us. I don't know who you have."

And Mac and Rosemary never did know who their guest was. Just a homeless dog. The story has a happy ending. The Kilduffs found the dog a home with a family who lived up the street from St. Thomas Church. I suspect that she was one of a group who barked at my arrival on Sunday mornings during the years I served there.

Somewhere below Mac Kilduff's humor there is a pervading sadness, for one day he found himself at the center of an event which brought great sadness on a nation and the world. I see it now and again in his eyes.

You have seen Mac Kilduff on TV. Every time someone comes up with a new theory on the assassination of President Kennedy, or an anniversary comes around, local and network TV interviewers look up Mac. You see, he was assistant press secretary under Pierre Salinger, and Salinger was somewhere else when the shots were fired in Dallas. You have seen film clips of a man with a cigarette hanging from his mouth, outside Parkland Hospital, waving TV cameras away. That was Mac. It was he who walked into a room and called Lyndon Johnson "Mr. President" for the first time, and it was he who made the official announcement to the world that his friend John Kennedy, who called him "MacDuff," was dead. In the photo of Johnson taking the oath on Air Force One, the hand holding the microphone is Mac's.

We were first stunned, and then began to despair, and I think Americans have never recovered from the horrors of that time and the time to follow, from the deaths of the President, Martin Luther King, Jr., and Robert Kennedy. And from the death of hope.

In his book *A Room Called Remember* Frederick Buechner wrote, "We are not only our own worst enemy, we are our only enemy."

Buechner tells of a day when he was traveling home and two images struck him. One was a cigarette ad on the train. Blue skies, young people enjoying themselves, and down in a corner of the ad the warning that cigarette smoking is dangerous. For the first time he realized that such ads really said, "Buy this: it will kill you."

A little while later he walked along New York's West 42nd Street among the porno shops and drunks and adolescent whores, seeing it all as if for the first time. He saw beneath our civilizedness, our religiousness, our humanness, that there is in all of us that which remains uncivilized, religionless, subhuman, "and which hungers for precisely the fare that 42nd Street offers, which is basically the license to be subhuman . . . to use and exploit and devour each other like savages, to devour and destroy our own sweet selves."

But there was a third image for Buechner that day. It was home, where his wife and daughter waited, where there was supper to be had, warmth, a cat asleep in front of the stove. It was a place of stillness, light, peace and love, an oasis in the desert "like the monasteries in the Dark Ages where truth, wisdom, charity, were kept alive surrounded by barbarity and mis-rule."

Now and then, Buechner wrote, we experience peace and love and light as he did that night at home; we should hold on to them because "they are glimpses and whispers from afar: that peace, light, love are where life ultimately comes from, that deeper down than madness and looseness they are what life at it's heart is. By faith we know this, and I think only by faith, because there is no other way to know it."

We need such lights in the darkness, places from which we go out to be Christ's in the world, and places toward which we invite the lost and wandering ones to come, to see the light, feel the warmth, enter into the peace of God.

The madness and lostness around and within us "are not the last truth about the world but only the next to the last truth," wrote Buechner. God made us "out of his peace to live in peace, out of his light to dwell in light, out of his love to be above all things loved and loving. This is the last truth about the world."

Leaving Cynthiana

Sundays at the Church of the Advent are one, two, three, and occasionally, four-train Sundays. The CSX track is a few feet from the back of the parish house and half a stone's-throw from the east end of the church. Trains blow their horns all the way through town. Readings and sermons stop until the engines pass.

Advent is in Cynthiana, Kentucky, about 70 miles south of Cincinnati, a little southeast of Hell's Half Acre and southwest of Devil's Backbone, places I've yet to visit. I came to Advent first in 1985 when my voice was almost gone and I could no longer do three Sunday services in my Lexington parish. I was there only a few months, serving part-time, when the Bishop decided to give Advent a full-time vicar.

When the vicar left in 1993 I let it be known that I was available Sunday mornings—and other occasions when needed. Our arrangement has continued for six years.

For years I was vaguely aware that there was a past family connection with Cynthiana. I learned that my Horine great-grandparents lived there for some time and two of their children were baptized at Advent. Whenever I minister at the font I think of them.

Episcopalians began meeting in Cynthiana in the 1830s. Some early baptisms were done in the Licking River, which flows north and empties into the Ohio opposite Cincinnati. Bishop Benjamin Bosworth Smith created the design for the Church of the Advent, using as his model Stoke Pogis Church in England, made famous by Thomas Gray's "Elegy Written in a Country Churchyard." The Cynthiana church is built of native stone. Construction began in 1854; the tower was finished in 1859. It's a beautiful old building.

During the Civil War there were a couple of hard battles at Cynthiana. For a time, the church was used as a hospital. Legend says that the rector during the war was a Union supporter and that many parishioners defected to the Presbyterians, who were Confederate sympathizers.

Advent's altar is a remarkable piece of work, carved in oak by women of the church in the nineteenth century. On the east wall, framing the altar, are the Apostles' Creed and the Ten Commandments in gold. The organ is more than a century old and was hand pumped until an electric blower was added in 1955. The stations of the cross were carved by young members of the church.

Cynthiana is the kind of place where traffic stops for a funeral procession. Downtown is still alive despite the Wal-Mart and other stores out on U.S. 27. Bianche's Restaurant has been in business for more than a hundred years.

I live 30 miles away, but feel at home in the church and the town, especially among the people of Advent. They are serious about the Lord's work, and who they are and what they do lovingly touches each other and the people throughout the community, and many beyond. During my time at Advent we have together offered the Eucharist each Sunday, celebrated births and baptisms and marriages, mourned the dead, and marked Independence Day with 1789 Evening Prayer, followed by a brass band concert and pie supper.

My goddaughter, Kate Darnell, serves as acolyte most Sundays.

I've stored up a lot of images. For instance, one

Christmas Eve two-year-old Allie Barnett escaped her parents in the back of the church, walked up the aisle in her red dress, and stood rapt as Deacon Linc Hartling read the prologue of John's Gospel. When he finished, she turned and walked back.

I'll be leaving the Church of the Advent in a few weeks because my body hurts. But that's nothing to how my heart hurts.

Flood of '97

There is a much-told little story that goes something like this:

A child who was afraid of the dark was told by his parents not to be afraid because God was with him. The child said that was okay as far as it went but he preferred the company of a God with skin on him.

I serve the Episcopal Church in Cynthiana, Kentucky, where the March flood put half the town under water. As I write this, hundreds of people are still unable to return to their homes. But people in Cynthiana have met God with some skin on him. Wherever somebody has helped another person, there was God with skin on.

In Lexington, where I live, we were lucky. We don't have a river. About the worst thing that could happen to us was flooded basements. My wife Becky and I had one of those. On Saturday, three feet of water put the furnace and the water heater out of commission and destroyed a lot of things that were intrinsically precious—pictures, notes, mementos.

The city sent out crews with hundreds of pumps and by Sunday noon the water level was down to a manageable level for our sump pump. By mid-morning on Monday the furnace and water heater were back in service and all that was left was to clean up the mess— tear up the carpet from my former office, throw out boxes of stuff that were beyond saving.

The people in Cynthiana dealt with problems that

were way beyond ours. They didn't have much time and energy for reflection, but I had a little.

On Tuesday I awoke and there was no rain falling and the first thing I heard was a bird singing. I immediately thought of some favorite lines from a Thomas Merton journal. Since I can't find it, I paraphrase: The rain ceases, the sun breaks through, and suddenly the song of a bird announces the Kingdom of God. It was one of those moments, a moment of thanksgiving. I had finally been in touch with Cynthiana by phone and had directions on how to get here by back roads.

I was also grateful for something that happened Saturday night. At dinner time we had trickles of water in the basement. We had put some things up on shelves so they wouldn't get wet. An hour later the water had started to rise quickly and was deep enough to make wading dangerous because there were live electrical appliances already under water. By bedtime it was a couple of feet deep.

I was mourning what I thought would be the certain loss of my sermons and most everything I had written over the past 30 years. We had put them up where we thought they would be safe, but now it appeared they would be in water before morning. I think I whined. Those papers, I said, were my life's work.

Since there was nothing else to do I went to bed. Becky stayed up. About a half hour later she came upstairs, wet from the waist down. She had gone into the water and carried what must have been a hundred pounds of papers out of the basement. I was not sure whether to kiss her or to ground her for risking her life. And I was torn between relief and guilt that my complaint about losing what I called my life's work had moved my wife to do such a gracious but foolish thing.

My life's work. Earlier on Saturday we had brought up a box of photographs that had been soaked already. As I spread them out to dry on Sunday I thought how wrong I was about my writing being my life's work. Here was pictures of people I had loved and served over the course of my ordained ministry—children I had baptized and watched grow up, families with whom I had lived through good and bad times. A couple of pictures of me when I had hair and funny glasses. No, I thought, it was not the writing I had done that was my life's work. It was this ministry among these people. It was my service to them, my ministry in their lives. That was my life's work.

I'm happy to say that this patriarchal view of my life's work was short-lived. Before the day was out I realized that neither my writing nor my particular ministry was my life's work. They were merely adjectives modifying the subject. My life's work was and is to live. That is my life's work. And your life's work. To live, to be with each other, to learn, to teach each other to be human. You see, brother bird's song announced the Kingdom of God because brother bird lives in that kingdom. He is exactly what God made him to be. We are not. We will all do different things with our different gifts, but our life's work is to be—and with God's help to become—human, gracefully to practice living the life offered to us in Christ Jesus. We spend our lives becoming real human beings as brother bird is—already—a real bird.

It was after this revelation that I opened the readings for the following Sunday and read these words from Ephesians: "But God, who is rich in mercy, out of the great love with which he loved us . . . made us alive together with Christ . . . and raised us up with him, and made us sit with him in the heavenly places . . . for we are his worksmanship, created in Christ Jesus for good works, which God prepared beforehand, that we should walk in them."

Our life's work includes among other things representing to each other God with skin on. In crises like that of the spring flood a standard theological question for reflection is, "Where was God in this; where can we find God in this?"

(Which reminds me of an old story passed down by old journalists back when I was one of them: When the unbelievable Johnstown flood occurred, newspapers rushed reporters to the scene. It was a time of florid, awful writing. One of the reporters telegraphed his editor a story that began something like this: "Today God sat on a hill looking at the devastation that once was Johnstown . . . " The editor immediately telegraphed the reporter: "Forget flood, interview God.")

God was in this flood with the victims and with the rescuers, the served and the servers. There is another piece from Thomas Merton that turned up in a box we retrieved from my office. A statement of faith for this and all times as we go about our life's work:

"My Lord God, I have no idea where I am going. I do not see the road ahead of me. I cannot know for certain where it will end. Nor do I really know myself, and the fact that I think I am following your will does not mean that I am actually doing so. But I believe that the desire to please you does in fact please you. And I hope I have that desire in all that I am doing. I hope that I will never do anything apart from that desire. And I know that if I do this you will lead me by the right road though I may know nothing about it. Therefore will I trust you always though I may seem to be lost and in the shadow of death. I will not fear, for you are ever with me, and you will never leave me to face my perils alone." (from *Thoughts in Solitude*)

PART 2

HOLY DAYS

Thanks for the Small Things

Gabrielle was the first cat in my life. She arrived as a well-intentioned but unexpected and unapproved birthday present for my daughter from one of her friends. Gabrielle soon charmed us all. Her personality matched her more or less Gaelic name. One minute she was a lover, caressing and purring; the next she was a spitfire daring a Rottweiler to enter her yard.

In cold weather, in the drafty old house where we then lived, Gabrielle climbed up on the back of my chair in the den to be as close as possible to the heat of my reading lamp. Later she began lying partly on the chair back and partly on my head. Since you lose a lot of your body heat through your head, and since my hair was already quite thin, this arrangement was satisfactory for us both. And there's something peaceful about a sleeping cat—in your lap or on your head.

I write this a week before Thanksgiving and I am totaling up things to be thankful for. One of them is this memory. A small thing. I am thankful for a lot of big things, like my family, and my work and my ability to do it, for the more than ample comforts and security of my life. But today I am thinking about "small" things:

- A hug at the church door from someone who has never done it before
- Reruns of the Bob Newhart Show

- Thirty minutes of silence
- An Agnus Dei that unexpectedly grabs my heart
- Small talk with friends over lunch at a neighborhood beanery
- A bride and groom exchanging vows, looking at each other with sudden deep understanding of the commitment of love they're making
- The blue cast of light at sunrise on a morning full of snow
- Discovering that someone whose opinion I respect also likes Willie Nelson
- A letter from a long-time-unheard-from friend
- Good news from my annual physical
- Coming across a neighbor in a distant airport (and other coincidences)
- Giving someone just the right thing at the right moment
- A man singing in the streets as he works
- The first look of recognition as my newest grandchild examines my face
- A morning when I wake early and lie in the warmth of our bed, watching my wife sleep

In all these times and events I have come across some sign of the love of God—generosity, beauty, peace, hilarity, humanity. Big things are important, but the small ones, the common, everyday ones may speak to us more directly and clearly of God's love and its echoes among us, God's children. The story of Elijah at the cave entrance helps me remember. While he waited for God, there was an earthquake, but God was not in the earthquake. Then came a great wind, but God was not in the wind. Next a fire, but God was not in the fire. God was not in any of the big stuff; when he came to Elijah it was in a small voice in the stillness. I need to listen more for the small voice and to take more notice of the small happenings in life. Looking down the weeks, I see a mighty king—a very important man—fretting in his palace about how to hold onto his power. And I see some ordinary people, who didn't matter much, from a town that didn't matter much, making their bed in a stable, which didn't matter much, and the woman having a baby, which wouldn't have mattered much except he was God.

Because God has come in this small way, everyone and everything and all that happens matters, and God's grace so fills this small world that grateful souls are joyfully overwhelmed with occasions for thanksgiving.

Traveling by Cow

Louise West told me this story years ago. Louise had grown up in a very small town in Mississippi. She was a teenager when this happened. One night she had been visiting at her sister's house, and when she went outside to go home she found that awful kind of darkness in which you really can't see your hand before your face.

But home was not far away and she figured it was a route she could follow blindfolded. And besides, there was a fence she could run her hand along as she walked, an aid to navigation, keeping her from straying.

Louise had walked some distance, running her hand along the fence to stay on the path, when, suddenly, she stepped over something. What she stepped over was a cow who was lying by the fence in the dark, taking her ease.

Now Louise was surprised to encounter the cow, but the cow was even more surprised to meet Louise. Unfortunately, Louise had got only one foot over the cow, so that when the animal, startled, raised up and ran off into the night, Louise was on the cow's back. The cow was bawling. Louise was screaming.

Neighbors, hearing the commotion, hurried to throw open their doors and come out to see what awful thing was happening. The open doors let out enough light to show Louise the way home, and having somehow dismounted, she went there directly.

That's what's needed on a dark night—some light to see your way by, some light to find your way home by.

In our cities the streets are lighted; in our homes we keep nightlights to protect us from skinning our shins on coffee tables and stepping on cats. We carry flashlights and lanterns. We don't like the dark, we don't trust the dark. The dark sometimes is frightening and sometimes dangerous.

The Lord is our light, in the darkness around us and the darkness within us. And we are the carriers of God's light to a darkened world. Christ said, "You are the light of the world."

Being the light means many things. It means, for instance, feeding the hungry; teaching the ignorant; sending aid when there has been a disaster. Politically and economically it means, in the words of the Prayer Book, making no peace with oppression. Being the light means bringing comfort to people who are suffering. And above all else it means seeing that people know they are loved by God and bringing them closer to him.

We carry the light wherever we go, whatever we're doing. And we may be the only light in someone's darkness.

In Advent we deal with the four last things—death, judgment, hell and heaven. I think of those open doors in Louise's town in Mississippi. Heaven is becoming eternally open to God and to each other. Open enough to light up hell itself.

"Arise, O Jerusalem, stand upon the height and look toward the east, and see your children gathered from west to east, at the word of the Holy One, rejoicing that God has remembered them. For God will lead Israel with joy, in the light of his glory, with the mercy and righteousness that come from him." (Baruch)

Colored Lights,
Happy Meetings

Early one evening about the middle of November as I was driving to my son's place, I was thinking that in another couple of weeks houses in the area would begin to show Christmas lights. No neighborhood does it any more elaborately than that one. Then I turned a corner and there they were, the first of the season, strings of colored lights outlining the porch and two huge lighted candles flanking the steps.

I drove on to my son's house with lightened spirits. I know it was too early, that one should decently wait until at least the day after Thanksgiving. I know that to be absolutely correct one should wait until Christmas Eve. But I get a lift out of Christmas lights, and if they're up a month or two prematurely, well . . .

My wife and I live on a dead-end street among people who take great pride in the neighborhood's appearance. We see that private yards are green and neat with just the right plantings, that a couple of small public areas are well tended, that trees are properly trimmed (and replaced when they get decrepit), that sidewalks are uncracked, that driveways are sealed before winter and that the street is closed to through traffic a couple of times a year for block parties.

We have a neighborhood association.

Recently the neighborhood news sheet was distributed. Among other items was the suggestion that houses display only white lights. The same suggestion was made last year. (I think there was also a date suggested for turning on such lights, but I threw the paper away and am not sure.) Last year a couple of free-thinkers put out colored lights. I'm counting on them again this year because my wife is a conformist and I am just plain timid where the neighborhood association is concerned.

I associate white lights with the more somber parts of Handel's "Messiah" and colored lights with the "Hallelujah Chorus." And with "Joy to the World" and "Jolly Old St. Nicholas." As the winter darkness deepens I think the latter are needed more than the former. The fact that people put out their lights earlier and earlier I claim as supporting evidence of their need for light and color and joy in the darkening season—and for some, I suspect, in dreary lives.

Advent was a happy time for me even before I had heard of it. When I was a kid, Christmas—not Advent; we were Methodists—began for me when the Lionel train display was set up in Purcell's department store and the America Flyer trains started running at Montgomery Ward. Occasions for joy. But the greatest event of late November-to-early-December was my father's homecoming. Pop worked for a tobacco processing company and spent months away each year. Some weeks before Christmas he came home for the winter. The morning he was due I got up really early because his train came in about 5 o'clock. I waited in the dark front hall forever. And then the street light would cast his silhouette on the front door's frosted glass and, Advent or not, at our house it was Christmas.

So in these weeks before Christmas, bare trees, shortening days, deepening cold, and the smell of tobacco actually bring me good feelings. And colored lights make me smile. They speak to my heart of happy meetings— of little ones at our front door, and of great ones with

God, some past, some now, some coming.

I am absolutely confident that if heaven has trees and decorates them to celebrate the coming of Christ all the lights will be colored and there will be a zillion of them.

Miss Marie

May you be strengthened with all power according to his glorious might, for all endurance and patience with joy, giving thanks to the Father, who has qualified us to share in the inheritance of the saints in light. He has delivered us from the dominion of darkness and transferred us to the kingdom of his beloved Son. (Colossians 1:11-14, RSV)

A year after I was ordained I was called as rector of St. Stephen's Church in the Latonia area of Covington, Kentucky. I was, as are many newish priests, full of myself and eager to convert everyone to the right way of being an Episcopalian (my way).

Bishop William R. Moody saved me from making a complete fool of myself by advising me to go to St. Stephen's and "just love the people." For some reason, or by grace, I listened to him and did that and they loved me in return.

Wonderful characters. Grace, who used to go out and talk with her garbage collectors, praising them for the good work they were doing. Mary, who, in the hospital with a life-threatening condition, would get out of bed to take me to some other patient who needed—she had decided—to see a priest. Bob, a shy man who gave generously and secretly from his limited income. Steve and Rick who became priests; Terry who is a deacon.

Another Mary. I thought of her one night as I drove through Latonia and glimpsed through winter-bare trees the now darkened house where she had lived. Mary—or

Marie. She called herself Mary; the people of St. Stephen's called her Miss Marie. When I arrived at the parish she was still substitute teaching in Covington schools, although she must have been near 80 by then. There were in the church grandparents she had taught in elementary school.

Occasionally Miss Marie would call me and say, "This is Mary Dunlap; my sister would like to see you when you have a chance." And that was about the extent of the conversation. It was some time before I realized she was very hard of hearing and had no idea what I said in response.

It was always, "My sister wants to see you." That was because her sister was "high church" and I was somewhere in that camp, according to Miss Marie. But when I arrived at the house it was Miss Marie who really wanted to talk. Often it was about who needed help and what could be done about it.

She was notorious as a driver. There were two pedals in her car—go and stop. The vehicle's sides were dented and had stripes of many colors from rubbing against garage walls and, I'm afraid, other cars. Once she asked me to go with her to a nursing home at the top of Kyles Lane, a treacherous, winding road. I must have gone pale, because she smiled—something she didn't often do—and said, "You can drive."

In my first services at St. Stephen's she startled me by disappearing. She didn't use a kneeler, and being short, she disappeared behind the pew whenever we prayed, then popped up again after the "Amen."

In later years she began to have blackouts. They were brief, and more than once when one happened in a public place she recovered and got away before the paramedics arrived. She had a horror of going to the hospital, believing they would never let her out. But at last she had to go live in a nursing home. Even there, nearing 100, she was champion wheelchair bowler.

Miss Marie told me many times she wanted me to bury her in the cemetery near the house in Lexington where she had been born. She didn't put the request in writing, but when at last she died the then-rector was unable to come to Lexington and asked me to do the service, and her wish was fulfilled. It was an occasion when those words from the burial office seemed most appropriate: "All of us go down to the dust; but even at the grave we make our song: Alleluia, Alleluia, Alleluia."

And so I remembered her that night as I drove down James Avenue. The house where she and her sister lived still sits at the end of Madison Court on a hillside overlooking Latonia. When Miss Marie lived there, all during Advent there were candles in every window of the big old place. (We were certain she would burn the house down.) Urban winters in this part of the country can be dreary—a reminder, perhaps, of the "dominion of darkness." But for many years the lights shone on that hillside, speaking to us of the coming of Christ, inviting us to claim our inheritance with the saints in light, who now number among them Miss Marie, who cared for minds and souls; Grace, who honored her garbage men; Bob, who gave alms quietly; Mary, guide of priests among the sick; and others who loved and taught each other to love, whose lives sang "Alleluia" and spread light.

Let It Snow!

Somebody came into my parish office one day, looked around, and said it looked more like a museum than a study.

I'm a collector. I like things. Some I like to handle, some I like to look at, some I use in my work. I know that possession of things can get out of hand so that things end up having you instead of the other way around. I also know that one can be tyrannized by a few things as easily as a lot.

I have a lot. Most of them are books. I am reasonably generous at lending them, but I can turn nasty when a beloved book disappears while it's on loan. It's not just possessiveness; if you need a book, I may give it to you for your very own. But when my books are out on loan I worry about them because they're old friends. We've spent time together, shared experiences, and when I meet them on the bookshelves we recognize each other.

In my study are books autographed by Bishop John Moorman, Malcolm Boyd, Elisabeth Kubler-Ross. There is an autograph of Archbishop Ramsey, a badge from my chaplaincy with a fire department, a walking stick carved by a teen-aged camper, and an ocean shell with a hole in it, put there when the same kid decided to come out of her shell.

Pipes, too. I collect pipes more than I smoke them. We've spent time together, too. This one came from a little town in Ontario, this one from Charleston, this one from San Francisco, this one from London, this from Dublin.

Here's one made from a piece of tree from Lookout Mountain, and it has a bullet lodged in it from that Civil War battle. It belonged to my great-grandfather, who was a Union cavalryman. And here's one of my grandfather's old corncobs. He puffed on it hour after hour as he rocked and read in the loneliness of his deafness. A dinner bell from my great-grandparents' farm. A toy car that belonged to my best friend, who died.

A lot of other stuff. If I had to throw some things away I guess I could, but I'd much rather find them good homes. Especially since all the places where we throw things away are filling up. (Rodney Dangerfield once asked how come you carry in two bags of groceries and produce from them three bags of garbage.)

Which brings me to a landfill. Not far from my first parish was a landfill that was still being filled. There were softball diamonds on part of it, but another part had a lot of ugly stuff—pieces of old cars, rotten chairs, scrap lumber with rusty nails—lots of rusty things, squishy things, things with sharp corners. Ugly.

Until it snowed. When snow came it covered the landfill and all its junk, all the ugliness. The rusty, squishy, sharp-cornered things were covered with a beautiful blanket of white, clean and smooth.

The ancients thought about things like that. The psalmist asked that God make him clean, as pure as snow. It was one of God's wonders, snow. In the book of Job there is a hymn to God's wisdom and omnipotence that says, "When He says to the snow, 'Fall on the earth' or tells the rain to pour down in torrents, He brings all men's strivings to a standstill so that each must acknowledge His hand at work."

It snows and all the ugliness with which people have maimed the earth is made to look pure again.

In weekly chapel services I used to tell day-school children that snow is a lot like God's love. If we throw away all the bad things, all the ugly things that are in us—the bad things we say and the bad things we do and the bad things we think—if we throw them out and say, "Here they are, God. I don't want them anymore," then God's love comes down and covers them up as the snow covers the landfill and makes life beautiful.

Just when we think we and the world are incurably ugly, God snows on our sins, even the ones we've always thought were too much even for God. He snows on our fears, even those of our worst imaginings. He snows on our grief, even grief we knew we couldn't live through.

All the ugly things, all the poison stuff, all the hurtful rubbish that we've kept out of timidity or cynicism or self-pity or despair; all the things that have piled up until they threaten to crush us—all these things we can throw out and God will send his snow, his love, to cover them, and make life beautiful as it's supposed to be.

Of course snow gets dirty and melts and there's the same old junk again, so here's where the analogy breaks down (if it hasn't already). Snow is cold and you can get hurt in it, but God's love is warm and healing and comforting, and it's not seasonal. The weather and the world may change, but God's love doesn't change.

Isaiah wrote, "Yes, as the rain and the snow come down from the heavens and do not return without watering the earth, making it yield and giving growth to provide seed for the sower and bread for the eating, so the word that goes from my mouth [says God] does not return to me empty, without carrying out my will and succeeding in what it was sent to do."

Beginning with Advent, we have been going through the season that reminds us that things are changing, that things that were old are being made new, and what was cast down is being raised up. Things are changing not only in appearance, but in truth.

Let it snow.

The Dog in the Snowstorm

I know what I want for Christmas — I want my childhood back. Nobody is going to give me that . . . I know it doesn't make sense, but since when is Christmas about sense, anyway? It is about a child of long ago and far away, and it is about a child of now. In you and me. Waiting behind the door of our hearts for something wonderful to happen.   —Robert Fulghum

"One Christmas was so much like the other in those years. I can never remember whether it snowed for six days and six nights when I was twelve or whether it snowed for twelve days and twelve nights when I was six."

Those are among the opening words of Dylan Thomas's "A Child's Christmas in Wales." There is a lot of snow in the story, and good food and drink, and a warm house and good company.

The reading of this little work has been one of our family Christmas customs for a long, long time, and as my years pile up I understand the poet's uncertainty in sorting out his Christmas memories. Images of long-ago Christmases run together in my memory, and there is always snow in them. I know better, but that's how I remember them.

Nearer memories are a little more reliable. When I was rector of my first parish there was snow. One Easter we had a lot of it. And at least one Christmas. The snow began on December 24 and it snowed and snowed. As the day went on, a fierce, cold wind began to drive the snow. In the afternoon we discovered a little dog curled up on the cushion of a wicker chair on the porch of the parish rectory.

I don't know how long he had been there, but he was shaking violently from the cold. I don't know why he had chosen our porch. We were two sets of steps up from the street and there were other, more accessible, better sheltered places available. I carried the dog upstairs to our apartment. We warmed him and fed him and while he rested we began trying to find his owner.

The dog had a license tag, but the animal shelter had closed at noon and it seemed there was no way to get him home. I thought about how I would feel if I lost my dog on Christmas Eve. Our one last try was a call to the police. Did they have access to dog license numbers? The policeman said the numbers were in an office that was locked for the holiday. I told him our story, and I guess it touched his heart. He said he would see what he could do.

When he called back a few minutes later, he had the name and address we needed. I didn't ask how he got the information from a locked room; I just thanked him and wished him a merry Christmas.

The little dog had wandered only a few blocks, and his owner came right away, a very happy man. It was our best present that Christmas, and one I've treasured through all the years since.

Winter is my favorite season, and especially if there is snow. I suspect winter is my favorite because Christmas is in it. Winter without Christmas would be pretty dismal. C.S. Lewis described his storyland of Narnia—under an evil spell—as always having winter, but never Christmas.

Some northern cultures have imagined hell not as a place of eternal fire, but of eternal cold. Hell is when you have wandered too far from God to find your way home, and you're lost in the dark and wind and cold and you know you're going to freeze to death and there's nothing you can do about it because you are alone.

Heaven is where they open the door and take you in out of the cold and warm you and feed you and give you rest and you find you are where you are supposed to be.

Christmas is about God coming into the cold with us to show us where to go, keep us company on the way, carry us if necessary, and bring us through the open door.

Red Socks at Christmas

How the wearing of the red socks began no one remembers. Like all real traditions it just came into being.

Sometime in the forties my father—Pop—and my Uncle Clarence—Monk—and I began to wear red socks on Christmas Eve. And we wore them in public. Late in the afternoon we put on our socks and walked downtown to Main Street, which had about a mile of stores and was as busy on Christmas Eve as the malls are now on the day after Thanksgiving.

We did our tour systematically, starting at the far end of the business district and working our way, store by store, both sides of the street, back to the end nearer home. Along the way we kidded with sales girls—they were, mostly, "girls," and in the first years, my early teens, I was practicing my flirting. We bought a last-minute present or two, stopped for a root beer, wished people along the way merry Christmas, and ended at the largest department store. There I had one last, lingering, lustful look at the great Lionel train layout that I had visited almost daily for a month. Then we walked the four blocks home, arriving in the early darkness tired, happy and hungry.

The church we belonged to in those days had its Christmas celebration on the Sunday before the holy day, and so we were at home on Christmas Eve. After supper my mother lit the two candles she had placed earlier in the day on the living room mantle. She played Christmas carols on the piano and all who were living in the rambling old out-of-plum family home sang. Pop, an intelligent man, able to do mysterious mathematical problems in his head and to design remarkably complicated machinery, never grasped the basic concept of music—that there are a number of tones that go up and down in a pattern. He sang loudest of all.

We sat near the tree—always a cedar with strings of lights that took turns failing—and we opened presents. Other family members and friends dropped by for Mom's fruitcake and a cup of eggnog. Old stories were retold, and there was more singing. Late at night we unplugged the tree, put out the candles and went to bed. I lay happily awake in what Dylan Thomas called the "close and holy darkness" until sleep overcame me.

I don't remember when we stopped our annual walking tour. Sometimes as the years passed Monk was absent, away in the Air Force. Then I was away in the Air Force. The last times we were together downtown my son Robert was big enough to go with us—wearing red socks. Then, little by little, there was no downtown.

Now on Christmas Eve, Robert, my daughter Ginny, their children and various in-laws carry on the socks tradition. And so do I, over the years giving countless acolytes moments of high glee when, as I kneel in the sanctuary, my alb slips aside revealing a flash of red.

There is no real point to this story—just red socks, a rememberance and symbol of thanks for shared joy and love, then and now and to the ages of ages, all the legacy of Mary's child.

A Little Story

Of all the powerful stories in the Bible, none surpasses this simple declaration: "While they were there the time came for her to have her child, and she gave birth to a son, her first-born. She wrapped him in swaddling clothes and laid him in a manger because there was no room for them at the inn" (Luke 2:6,7).

A little story . . . about the most wonderful thing that ever happened. This is another little story:

A week before Christmas one year I called on Miss Lucy and Miss Erma, elderly sisters and members of my parish, to give them communion and to visit for awhile. We naturally talked about Christmas and I asked them about Christmas memories. Miss Lucy and Miss Erma talked in general terms about how the holiday had been celebrated when they were younger and the family was still together.

After a time the two sisters sat for some moments in silence remembering. Then Miss Erma began to speak. She had been a teacher for forty years, most of them in first grade at one of Lexington's tougher schools. She talked about decorating her classroom, helping her children get ready for Christmas. She talked about those details for a few minutes and then she smiled and said that a friend had taken her shopping a few days ago and some men she had taught had seen her, recognized her as their first grade teacher, and greeted her warmly.

She sat back in her chair, obviously recalling

something special. She was looking far away when she said, "You know, I only spanked one child during those forty years."

He was much older and bigger than the little first graders. He had started out in a higher grade and had been put down step by step until he found himself in the lowest grade of all, with those he considered babies.

Left in Miss Erma's room, he went berserk. He tore pictures from the walls and threw them; he rampaged like an enraged animal, lashing out at anything his hands and feet found; he screamed obscenities, and finally he picked up a child and threw him across the room, miraculously doing no serious injury.

Miss Erma was a tall woman, but didn't give the impression of having been particularly muscular. Nevertheless, as the boy came near the door of the cloak-room, she grabbed him by the collar, flung him inside, followed after him, pulled him from the floor, sat on a bench, laid him across her lap and gave him five of the best across his bottom.

He cried. She said, "I knew when he started crying that something had happened." "Nobody's ever whipped me before," the boy said tearfully.

(It *had* hurt her more than it had hurt him.)

She sat him down and told him that if he wanted to get out of the first grade she would stay with him after school and help him learn. If he stayed that afternoon, she would know that's what he wanted.

When school was out, there he sat. Her eyes filled with tears as she remembered that moment. Day after day she stayed with him until six o'clock, teaching him what he needed to know to be promoted. Before the year was out the child was in the fourth grade. And he went on from there.

Agape, that extraordinary, special, selfless love—love not bounded by emotion but rooted in God-graced will—tells us about a connection unseen, from which we draw our humanity, which makes sense of all the other qualities that help make life interesting, exciting, fulfilling.

The person who loves extraordinarily is not an aberration, but one who is more fully human, one who is nearer to being what we are meant to be.

"All that came to be was alive with his life, and that life was the light of men." So wrote John (1:4 NEB). All came to be alive with his life, whether the creatures are aware of it or not.

It may be that God became one of us not only to show us what he is like, not only to show us how to live, but to show us why we do some good things, loving things, even before we know who he is. Maybe God came to show us that he had been at work already even in people who would say, "I never heard of God," if they have cared, if sometime they have offered something of themselves to another person. God comes quietly to live, to fill the emptiness within us, and the emptiness among his children.

"The light shines on in the dark, and the darkness has never quenched it."

Years later the wild kid from the first grade happily remembered the first spanking for either of them, remembered with love the one person who cared enough to get his attention and turn him around, remembered with love the first person, perhaps, who ever said in any way that he was important.

I suppose it would make a good story if I could tell you that the little boy Miss Erma spanked and taught and loved went on to become governor of the commonwealth, or president of IBM, or the discoverer of the polio vaccine. But the fact is that one day as Miss Erma walked along the street a milk truck pulled up to the curb, and the driver jumped down and ran over and gave her a hug. A life offered, a life saved; love given, love received, love remembered.

Maybe that's a better story, a story about a school teacher and a boy who grew up to be a milkman—a little story, like one about a baby born in a stable, sleeping in a manger.

Christmas is a little story that tells us about Jesus, about God, and about ourselves.

Love Is a Policy

Driving down the coast of Maine, we pulled off the highway at a tourist-baiting store in a village north of Camden. Over the hill before us came a pickup truck with red lights flashing behind its grill. The truck turned into a lane beside the store. Presently another pickup truck followed, and not a minute later we heard a deep-throated siren and a fire truck appeared in the lane and with a clash of gears pulled onto US 1 and disappeared over a rise to the north.

Minutes later a fire truck from a station further south passed and then we heard the siren of a third west of us on a parallel road. Volunteer firemen, all going somewhere because somebody or somebody's property was in danger.

Volunteer fire departments are remarkable institutions. When the call comes there are no questions to determine whether the caller is a deserving person; the firemen want to know only what the trouble is and where it is. I don't know whether volunteer departments are peculiarly American, but they symbolize something of the best of us—volunteers—people helping others not for money but because help is needed.

Years ago I knew a man who was, in the manner in which he presented himself to the world, a most selfish person. But when the town's fire siren went off he changed persona as quickly as Clark Kent ever did and dragged hoses and climbed ladders and chopped holes and did all the things firemen do. He would, I do not doubt, have gone into a blazing hell to rescue someone if it came to that. After the fire he was once again Clark Kent's unlikeable twin.

Home from Maine I searched out a copy of Kurt Vonnegut's *God Bless You, Mr. Rosewater* and found a passage I had read first long ago. In the book Eliot Rosewater is a multi-millionaire who answers the phone "The Rosewater Foundation, how can we help you?" People think he's nuts. Kilgore Trout assures him he's not:

"Your devotion to volunteer fire departments is very sane, too, Eliot, for they are, when the alarm goes off, almost the only examples of enthusiastic unselfishness to be seen in this land. They rush to the rescue of any human being, and count not the cost. The most contemptible man in the town, should his contemptible house catch fire, will see his enemies put the fire out. And, as he pokes through the ashes for remains of his contemptible possessions, he will be comforted and pitied by no less than the fire chief."

Vonnegut may not have intended it, but I read this as being about God's Love and the Incarnation and us. That familiar passage from John's Gospel begins, "God so loved the world . . ." The world was then, before Jesus, and is now, populated by people who are sometimes pretty good, sometimes not so good and sometimes downright contemptible. God loved and loves all of them—us.

Jayber Crow is the title and the narrator's name in Wendell Berry's new novel. Jayber, having fallen deeply in love, is trying to put a name on the love John's Gospel said God had for the world:

"I imagined that the right name might be Father, and I imagined all that the name might imply: the love, the compassion, the taking offense, the disappointment, the anger, the bearing of wounds, the weeping of tears, the forgiveness, the suffering unto death. If love could force my own thoughts over the edge of the world and out of time, then could I not see how even divine omnipotence might by the force of its own love be swayed down into the world? Could I not see how it might, because it could know its creatures only by compassion, put on mortal flesh, become a man, and walk among us, assume our nature and our fate, suffer our faults and our death?"

I once knew a man who kept a small, lighted Christmas tree in his bedroom. His work had taken him on the road a lot, and one year his wife had given him the tree to take with him during the weeks around Christmas. He became fond of the tree; it reminded him of home and was comforting on some dark, cold and lonely nights. When he retired he kept the tree where he could see it every day. He said it gave him warm feelings, but more than that, it reminded him to try to do what people often talk about in December and forget in January—to make every day Christmas.

He said he liked the feelings but he knew every Christmas was not about feelings, but about God's great Love and our reflecting that Love in everyday life. He said that Love is not a feeling, "It's a policy."

I think, at heart, he was a volunteer fireman.

Recognizing Terry

As I emerged from the dairy aisle in the neighborhood supermarket and turned toward the bagels, I spotted my old friend Terry Regan over near the soups. He saw me at the same time and we started toward each other. I hadn't seen Terry for nearly a year and he looked slimmer. Good for him, I thought; he needed to trim down a little.

We were grinning and had our hands stuck out to shake when I realized this wasn't Terry Regan. This wasn't anyone I knew at all. Still, our hands were out there and so we went on with the handshake and I said, "I'm Bob Horine. I thought you were someone else, but you're not. Who did you think I was?" Still grinning and shaking his head he said, "I don't know who I thought you were."

He introduced himself as Bob Halberson. Then he said, "Horine? Were you kin to Monk Horine?" (No one ever called my Uncle Monk by his real name, Clarence Calhoun.) Monk was a dozen years older than I, and Bob Halberson, I learned, was one of his high school classmates. He had been at Monk's military funeral and did a critique of the service. Poorest playing of taps he had ever heard, and the sailors having to refold the flag several times before they got it right was a sorry spectacle.

After we got past the funeral Bob told me stories from high school days and then moved on to tell about his time in the Navy. He had wanted to be a Navy pilot, but said he did so poorly he was given the option of becoming an ordinary U.S. sailor or joining the Japanese Navy. Bob talked for fifteen or twenty minutes until I had to leave to keep an appointment.

I've made other mistakes in identity. Once, in high school, I talked to a boy who was trying to move in on my girlfriend. I finished what I had to say and left him standing in the hall, speechless. No wonder. Wrong boy. Well, there are, after all, only so many faces to be shared among six billion people.

Recognizing people can be tricky business. After the Resurrection Mary Magdalene mistook Jesus for the gardener, the travelers to Emmaus didn't recognize Jesus until he had broken bread with them, and the disciples fishing in the early light weren't sure of identity of the man on the beach until Peter said, "It is the Lord!"

On Ash Wednesday my wife was delayed in getting to church. The imposition of ashes had been done. I was waiting in a back pew when she arrived. As if we had planned it, she turned to me and I took the ashes from my forehead and made the sign of the cross on hers, saying "Remember that you are dust, and to dust you shall return." In that moment I saw my wife in a way I cannot describe except to say it was a deeper kind of recognition, a discovery, a knowing beyond my experience of her through all the years of our life together.

Just before Easter I had a dream. Two friends were talking and in the middle of the conversation the world ended and they were changed and one said, seeing her friend clearly for the first time, "I had no idea!"—no idea of her true nature, the miracle of her friend's being, and of her own. The friends were seeing each other for the first time without the dark glass that obscures our mortal vision.

We are all connected because we are of the same stuff—"the dust contemplating itself," Teilhard de Chardin said—outcroppings of earth destined by God to become immortal spirit. How differently we might treat each other if we could always recognize every person in that way. How humbling to be aware of our common origin and our dependence on God for life. And how outrageously wonderful to see that God can do such things with a little dust—that he can and did and does and will.

We do get glimpses, now and then, here and there, maybe in church, maybe between the milk and the bagels.

Fire Pink

In the mid-forties William R. Moody became chief pastor of the Diocese of Lexington and set out to bring order, establish unity, and reawaken a sense of mission in a struggling church.

Among other acts, the bishop re-opened the diocesan seminary, closed since the Civil War; sent its graduates into vacant churches in rural areas, and began opening new missions. The legend is that he would call a man into his office, hand him a five-dollar bill, and say "Go start a church in . . ." and they did it.

His master stroke was the founding of a cathedral, surrounded by a camp and conference center in the hills of Lee County, the geographic center of the diocese. There were some strange and wonderful adventures in the building of the place. Once a tornado tore through the railway yard at nearby Ravenna where the lumber for the buildings had just arrived. Once when Bishop Moody spent the night in one of the first cabins there was a terrifying thunderstorm with lightning striking all around. The next morning he learned that there were several boxes of dynamite stored under the episcopal bed.

I wish I had been there when the bishop with his clergy spent a night in prayerful vigil and at dawn he raised his staff and pointed to the rising sun, fixing the position of the Cathedral of St. George the Martyr. He declared the last Sunday in April each year St. George's Day and invited everyone in the diocese to come and celebrate. They come by the hundreds every year.

Children and young people from throughout the diocese came to the summer camps. Now their children's children come. There's no place in the diocese where the mention of the Cathedral Domain doesn't bring smiles and misty eyes. I couldn't begin to tell you the stories former campers have told me about their experiences of the holy in that place. I'm not sure I could tell you all of mine. But I will tell two.

My introduction to the Domain came during the annual seminarians' retreat just before school opened in the fall. There was a "tradition" that the middlers lead the juniors in the dark up a rocky hill called Patterson, after a saintly priest who had traipsed Lee County preaching and baptizing a few decades earlier. Guardian angels were overworked on those nights. Seen in the daytime, Patterson was more like a southwestern mesa than one of Eastern Kentucky's gentle hills.

We climbed to the top. Mist lay in all the low places, so the hilltops were like islands in the moonlight. For a long time we sat in silent prayer, and then we came down and went to bed. I have never made that climb again, but I have often closed my eyes and been there once more.

Then there is the fire pink, a little red wildflower that begins to grow in the cool dampness of early spring in the Kentucky highlands and by St. George's Day gives bright patches of the saint's color to the green hillsides. More than dogwood and redbud it speaks to me of springtime, and more than lilies the red flowers whispering in the mountain breezes tell me of God's love, and the holiness of the place, and the promise of resurrection.

Wildflowers, wild mountains, wild rivers, wild deserts. Jesus in the desert; we in the desert of Lent. Places of wildness, places of solitude let us come closer to their Creator than those we have tamed, cultured, adapted, harnessed, conditioned, compromised, ravished. And there is something in us, some vestige still of the wild—

vestige of the creature we are meant by God to be.

We are not all yet entirely bound by our willfulness, and it is through the remaining wildness, naturalness of spirit that we can sometimes still hear God speak to us. It is through that remaining wildness of spirit that now and then we look not at, but through the wild things and wild places of the world—something so big as a mountain, something so vast as a desert, something so small as a fire pink—and dimly remember Eden, regret a world lost, look with compassion on the confusing struggles of the world in which we live, and enter into joy in anticipation of a world to come.

Reading in
the Cemetery

In the late 1940's there was still an establishment on the main street of Goldsboro, North Carolina that sold mules and horses. Saturday nights a crowd gathered in front of the news stand to listen to "Grand Ol' Opry" over a loudspeaker. When someone talked about "veterans" it was possible they were talking about survivors of the Civil War. For many people that war was only a generation removed. The fathers of some older people had fought for the Confederacy; the parents of others had been slaves.

Three or four times during those years my mother and I spent a couple of weeks visiting my father, who was there for the tobacco season. We stayed in boarding houses run by proper, elderly southern ladies, and I learned to eat grits and collard greens and field peas and that iced tea was always sweetened.

It was while we were sitting on the porch one summer evening, waiting to be called to the dinner table, that someone called our attention to the woman who walked past every day about the same time carrying her parasol and a newspaper. Sometime later she would pass in the other direction. Every day she walked to the cemetery, sat by her husband's grave and read him the *Goldsboro News-Argus*.

At the time I just thought what she did was peculiar. Why would she do it? Surely she knew he wasn't there.

Now, forty-some years later, I think I understand. She made that daily trip for herself. Her husband was dead and she needed to do something about it and this was the only thing she could think of. She identified her husband with his body.

I wonder whether she went on with her visits day after day, year after year, in East Carolina's muggy summers and cold, damp winters until they laid her body in a grave beside her husband's. I wonder if anyone ever told her about Mary Magdalene, another woman who identified her loved one with his body and came to tend it only to discover that he wasn't there. I wonder whether anyone ever told her what those who follow Jesus believe—that for all who enter the grave, in whatever place, in whatever time, there is a way out, through the tomb Mary found empty 20 centuries ago.

Grandpa's Watch

Easter seals God's promise that he cares for us, that he will look after us, that the mess we make of our lives, the mess we make of our world, will be changed, renewed.

My Aunt Jo died in December. I saw her often in the last days of her life. At the end, as throughout her life, she gave our family a wonderful gift—her confidence and faith in the God who showed himself to us in the person of Jesus Christ.

Saddened as we were by her suffering and death, we were filled with wonder, and if I were a poet I would write about days and nights in which her bed was surrounded by angels and archangels and in which Jo was in communion with all the company of heaven.

Jo gave me another gift, a material one, a gold watch that had belonged to my grandfather and before that to his uncle and before that no one knows. A beautiful piece of work. When Jo gave it to me it was running. However, the hands indicated the wrong time, several hours fast— or slow.

I pulled on the stem so I could move the hands to the right time, but the stem wouldn't pull out. I couldn't stop it or change the time. The hands continued to turn as they had done through at least four generations.

I recalled a short story I had read years ago about a man going about everyday activities when suddenly something very strange begins to happen. For instance, he might be reading the newspaper and time reverses for a short period: he lives backward. Then time resumes moving forward as usual. He is puzzled and astounded. All at once the movement of time, which we take for granted, can't be trusted.

The periods of living backward begin to come more frequently and last longer. Finally he lives back to the day when he and his wife had had a terrible argument, and she had driven away from home while both were angry. She had been in a wreck and died without any opportunity for them to heal the rift in their marriage, to recall their love for each other, to say goodbye.

The story has a happy ending. The man's life picks up momentum and runs back to the time of the argument. He defuses the situation and his wife doesn't leave and her life and their lives are saved.

A good story, but not the way things are. The watch's hands move inevitably on and we can't stop them or slow them or turn time back or forward.

But oh, if we could.

Is there anyone beyond childhood who wouldn't give up treasures to go back to a certain time and with knowledge of what might be, act in a different way, refrain from doing something that brought pain or grief or shame or separation—something that changed our lives or the lives of people we loved? Is there anyone beyond childhood who would not redo some moment of regret?

We all carry the memories of such moments. They are wounds, great or less great, that still give us twinges in the weather changes of the soul.

Bishop Addison Hosea taught the awful truth that if we once stole anything we became a thief and would so remain. Likewise with lying, or adultery, or murder. Once done, we had labeled ourselves by our sins. Not very comforting, and his students often argued with him about that teaching.

What can't be denied is that what we have done we can't undo. I passed a church bulletin board one day which said, "Time and words cannot be re-called." That's right, they can't.

God doesn't promise that we can rewrite our personal histories. God doesn't promise that a sinner can become a non-sinner. God promises that we sinners are forgiven.

We are God's children, wonderful creatures, but unable to save ourselves from ourselves. Our heart's cry, wrote St. Paul, is for "Abba," for our Father. And our Father comes to us and comforts us and takes the pain we give and the pain we bear into himself and at last brings us home, into his kingdom, into heaven, restored to life.

That's a promise.

An Early Easter
for Nolan

Give us grace to heed [the prophets'] warnings and forsake our sins, that we may greet with joy the coming of Jesus Christ our Redeemer. (The Book of Common Prayer, Collect for the Second Sunday of Advent)

One day when I was about ten, a boy my age came riding up on his bike and stopped to talk. From that day until we were in our late teens Nolan Puckett was my best friend and I was his. Even when his parents moved away to a farm in Indiana we never lost touch, and every summer Nolan would come to Lexington, find a job, and we would spend three months together. Nolan hated living on a farm so far from Lexington, and the night he graduated from high school we loaded his things in my car and he left Indiana for good.

In those growing-up years we were together during every waking hour. We were born during the Depression, and like many others of that age had no sisters or brothers. But Nolan and I were brothers-in-truth and we lived in each other's houses and ate at each other's tables naturally and got along a lot better than many brothers-in-fact did.

We shared just about everything—food, clothes, money and, occasionally, the love for and of a girl. Nolan was with me the day I bought my first car, a 1928 Chevrolet with little roof and less floorboard, for $45, and he was with me when my father made me take it back.

Although he was a Seventh-Day Adventist, we learned to smoke together, and I guess I helped him to break a number of other religious laws against Cokes, coffee, comic books and movies. I was a nominal Methodist, but I was probably in his church more often than my own. His parents were very devout and kept a strict sabbath from sundown Friday to sundown Saturday. Those sabbaths were trying days because Nolan wasn't allowed to do much of anything except go to church meetings and have family prayer and Bible study.

Church was, for us, something to be endured and we simply made the best of it. Often that meant embarrassment for his parents and ourselves. We found a lot to snicker about in church, usually when there was a foot-washing or one of us was called upon to say a prayer. We laughed and laughed through our childhood years, once to our great surprise and shame during visitation in a funeral home.

We played pranks, and those using the telephone were among our favorites—"Do you have Prince Albert in the can?" "Is your refrigerator running?" "We're testing telephones; would you stand back six feet and whistle?" Once Nolan picked a number at random from the phone book, and reached an elderly man and convinced him that they knew each other. It was kind of funny at the time, but something led Nolan to call the old man at other times, and they would carry on long conversations. I think Nolan was touched by a loneliness he sensed at the other end of the line.

As younger boys, we haunted Woolworth's and Kresge's. When we fought we fought with other kids, never with each other. Later we spent long evenings in drugstores, parks and drive-in restaurants where girls were to be met. We mowed lawns, worked as bag boys for Kroger, or jerked sodas for gasoline money. We knew every street and alley in Lexington, and in our teen years walked miles of them after midnight, our car often being indisposed. We missed lots of last busses and as we walked we sang, not very well perhaps, but with heart. I remember one night walking down the middle of normally busy Central Avenue singing "Good Night Irene." We sang with the gusto of youth, happy and excited with living.

I guess we figured life would go on like that forever, but I went to college, the Air Force and marriage and Nolan went to the Army, Korea, marriage, and a long stream of jobs in a long string of cities. We lived in different places, had different interests, raised children, and heard from each other less and less frequently until at last we only heard about each other through other people.

And then in January of 1991 my father died and Nolan came to the funeral home and hugged me and I didn't know at first who he was. I hadn't seen him for 20 years or more. He stayed around for awhile, and we were sort of awkward in our conversation, and then he left.

It was two or three months later that my mother called me to tell me that Nolan was in the VA hospital and had cancer. I went to see him pretty much every week. We remembered old times and laughed. Then one day he told me he had six months to a year to live. And we began to talk of other things—of fear and grief and regret and doubt and things unfinished—but more about faith. And we still laughed sometimes. Once we laughed because I told him I thought he would pass right through death into new life and he said he didn't think so, but he would be "dead as a doornail" until resurrection day.

In the fall Nolan went home to Lawrenceburg, Kentucky, to wait. Sometime before Christmas he told me he had asked a friend to drive him to Indiana to see the farm. His parents had died years ago and the government had bought the land. He found it fenced off and overgrown with weeds. The house and outbuildings were gone. I wondered why he made the trip. He wondered too. He had never liked living there. But this is what I think: it had been the last safe place in his life. Despite his old time feelings, it was his last real home. And it was for him a reminder of the home for which we all long, have never seen, and have heard of only in our hearts.

His trip was about our journey into eternity and our Lord coming to meet us while we are still on the way. Nolan made the trip during Advent, that bittersweet time in which we find ourselves somewhere between birth and death, sad at the leavings, sorry for the things that didn't go right, but living with hope, expectation, and great joy in the anticipation that grows within us as the time of meeting comes closer—first week by week, then day by day, then hour by hour until we know the reality of those words from the Christmas Collect, "that we, who have known the mystery of that Light on earth, may also enjoy him perfectly in heaven."

Nolan stayed at home with his children during Christmas, then chose to return to the hospital. On a Saturday night in January his son called to tell me his dad was near death. I sat with Nolan and his children into the early hours of Sunday.

I have always been suspicious of the authenticity of elaborate and quotable "last words." Only those of Jesus—and those like them—seem to ring true. Nolan, fighting for breath, managed to say only two things that I remember. Once he raised himself a few inches off the pillow and said, quite simply, "I believe." When I had to leave the hospital for awhile, I touched him and said, "Nolan, I have to go for awhile. I'll see you either here or there." He said, "Okay" with the same confidence he had said "I believe." He died two hours later.

On Tuesday I sat with the pallbearers in a Lawrenceburg funeral home chapel and listened to the music Nolan had selected for the occasion. I was surprised to hear a classical piece among the familiar hymns. When we were kids the only thing we disagreed about was music. Nolan was a devout country music fan; I followed the straight pop line. After all the preaching and praying were finished, Nolan's last request was playing. It was "The Tennessee Waltz." I didn't laugh, but I smiled hard.

Our theological differences aside, I believe Nolan's Easter came early that year.

PART 3

saints

Holding Hands

Awhile back Forward Movement Publications staff members spent a get-away day at the Convent of the Transfiguration in Glendale, Ohio, to think, make plans, talk about dreams.

The Reverend Edward S. Gleason, FMP's director and editor, and I began the day by attending the Eucharist with children from Bethany School, which makes its home on convent grounds. I expected to sit at the back of the chapel, but a sister seated us higher up in the middle of a sea of animal energy I felt was barely contained by school uniforms, a handful of hard-learned rules of civilization and the presence of teachers at the ends of each pew.

It turned out well. The kids read lessons, served the altar and led some of the singing. There were familiar hymns, but also some songs that might be sung at camp or Cursillo. One was "His Banner Over Me Is Love," which calls for doing things with your body as you sing. I'm no good at this kind of thing. I never stand up or sit down when I'm supposed to and I'm always afraid I'll poke myself in the eye. Ted Gleason, on the other hand, a big man, was as coordinated as a ballerina.

We finally got to a place in the song where I could safely take part. We held hands with the people on each side of us, and as we did I remembered being a little kid in the first grade and at the direction of the teacher unselfconsciously holding hands with a girl or a boy when the class took a walk—a "field trip."

Later I thought of other hand-holding. I remembered sitting in the balcony of a movie house holding the hand of my first serious girlfriend until the sweat ran down our fingers. I remembered holding my father's hand on the last day of his life. I remember holding my wife's hand and making promises about our life together. I remembered a strange incident during a period of considerable stress years ago; I was praying and it was as if someone took my hand and held it for awhile.

I remembered the memorial service for a friend—Geri, a scholar, an athlete, a faithful Christian—who began a rapid descent into Alzheimer's Disease at 50 and lived there for seven years.

Her death moved me to think about what gives life meaning. In the first years of my priesthood I had quick answers for every question.

Gradually my early knowledge and "wisdom" shrank as I began to see something of the unfathomable Love in which we live—with God and with each other. The most articulate theologian comes no nearer defining that love than does my youngest granddaughter singing the ABC song.

At Geri's memorial service I sat next to the aisle near the back of the church. As the procession left the nave, her husband and other old friends reached out and took my hand. These were more than handshakes. They had to do with who we are and whose we are. They were a sign of recognition, an acknowledgement of something we know but have no words to tell.

At a meeting I attended, the Rt. Rev. J. Clark Grew, Bishop of Ohio, mentioned an experience that caught my attention. Later I asked him to tell the whole story.

Bishop Grew was making his annual visit to an inner city, charismatic parish. The 10 o'clock service had a lot of worshipful preliminaries so that it was nearly 11 before they got to "Blessed be God, Father, Son and Holy Spirit." It was not the sort of service the Bishop was accustomed to and he was a little uneasy about the outcome. His words follow:

"Somewhere during the Liturgy of the Word, a young girl, probably six or seven, moved from the congregation to the sanctuary and sat next to me. She wanted to hold my hand, but she didn't speak. She remained in that seat while I preached, but for the rest of the service she never left my side. During the laying-on-of-hands, which ended up including the entire congregation and took about forty minutes, she stood next to me and watched. As soon as I was done, she reached for my hand. When I passed the Peace with parishioners so did she. I realized, as I sat down after the offertory sentences, once again holding hands, that the anxiety lodged in my spirit at the start of worship had been replaced by a deep sense of wonder— this child, this hand, this service, this grace—all of it wrapped in some way with my own salvation.

"Just prior to the Great Thanksgiving, the girl leaned over and asked if I was about to go somewhere. I think she sensed a change in the rhythm of things. I whispered to her that I had to go to work now, but that I would be back. She remained in the chair—and left the service in procession, hand-in-hand with me.

"I have not seen her since. I am embarrassed I can't remember her name. When I asked about her after the service, the rector told me that her mother, who was in church that morning, was going to prison on Monday to serve a sentence for shoplifting. The girl's father left a long time ago."

Do you remember the song, "Put your hand in the hand of the man who stilled the waters; put your hand in the hand of the man from Galilee . . . ?" Maybe all this can be wrapped up in a parable. All Jesus' parables were about the Kingdom of God. So our parable might be: Entering the Kingdom of God is like a first-grade class taking a walk with the teacher. Everyone holds hands and we walk together until we get there.

Love Song

Several months after my voice had gone bad, I made a visit to Israel. By that time I had become used to having little voice and little control over what I did have. One day we were, as I remember, near Jerusalem's Sheep Gate and stopped in a church. I think it was St. Anne's. There was a service going on with spirited singing. For some reason I joined in like I knew what I was doing, and behold: I could sing! So I did, at the top of my lungs, and went away feeling great happiness.

From that same trip I have an image I can go back to as if it were just happening. I am standing in the back of a boat crossing Lake Galilee. There are rays of sunshine through clouds, like a pretty good 19th century religious picture, and a gull wings across the scene; I break into singing a canticle of praise. The noise of the boat's engine and the rush of the wind cover my offering so it is just between me and God.

So, I learned that although I couldn't talk well, I could sing. When I later met other people with my problem, I learned that many of them did likewise. I also learned that it was costly to sing. It takes great effort because one uses a lot more air than normal people and strains muscles. If I sing a lot it knocks my voice out for a day or two. Nevertheless, sometimes I do it.

Usually not. Maybe Easter and Christmas. But while I don't always sing with my outward and audible voice, I can sing with an inner one. And I have a certain advantage. I can sing like Pavorotti with that voice. Or I can be a baritone. Or I can sing all the parts at the same time. My inner voice is not limited.

I'm going to tell you three little stories about singing.

My daughter-in-law Donna for years was a social worker at St. Elizabeth Hospital South in Northern Kentucky. She told me about Sister Valeria, an aged nun who was assigned chaplaincy duties in the pediatric section. Donna said the nun was a "good soul" and effective in her work, although her methods were not those used by younger "more professional" chaplains.

She walked among the children carrying two ancient toy donkeys with bobbing heads, which delighted the children. Once in the emergency room she sat down beside a distraught woman and said, "Would you like to put your head in my lap?" and the woman did and was comforted.

Perhaps because of her old-fashioned ways, Sister Valeria was told she was being retired. When people asked why she was leaving, she wouldn't talk, although she said it would come out on Judgment Day. But on her last day at the hospital she told some employees, "Remember, you're not allowed to sing in the hallways anymore."

The second story is also from a hospital, St. Joseph's in Lexington. When I married, one of the fringe benefits was getting to be friends with my wife's friends. One of the most remarkable people I know is Sara Holroyd, who was director of choral music at the University of Kentucky until she retired a few years ago. Sara retired and went back to school to become a registered nurse. She works in St. Joseph's emergency room, which like all city emergency rooms often has a stressful atmosphere.

One day an ambulance brought in a 98-year-old man from Lee County in the hills east of Lexington. He was scared and confused and very hard of hearing. Sara needed to insert an IV and catheterize the old man, but he was thrashing around calling, "Oh God, oh God have mercy, God help me, oh God!" Sara came near his good ear and said, "Mr. Burgess, God told me he wants you to be a little quieter." That helped, and then as she worked with him she began to sing old-time hymns to him. The emergency room got quiet and people in that busy place listened, and some wept, and Mr. Burgess and others were comforted.

In his book, *The Silent Self: A Journal of Spiritual Discovery,* George A. Benson tells about his walk through Nepal. He came across an old Napalese couple plowing on a poor little farm. The man pulled the plow and the woman guided it. It was a pitiful picture of poverty and hopelessness. But in the evening Dr. Benson saw the old people again at the village spring. The woman was stripped to the waist and the old man was washing her back. He remembered that while they plowed the woman sang to the man. He wrote, "What, then, did the Nepalese couple have that separated them from the inherent travail of existence? I believe that they had one further piece of knowledge; they knew that they were more than themselves. They knew that beneath and beyond their humanity there is a singing God."

We are more than ourselves and we are more than we ordinarily realize. We are made in the image of the singing God. Some people's lives really sing. Our calendar lists a few of them. They sing a song that is in harmony with the song of God. God's song is a love song. Their hearts sing with God's heart, and in the harmony comes God's peace.

When we sing this love song other people hear with their hearts and join in. What a chorus! If we keep singing maybe the world's hard-of-hearing may yet hear God's song and God's peace will bring the world peace.

Called to Remember

Those of us who come from south of the Ohio River grant honorary kinship to people we love who are not related by blood. We grew up with such cousins and uncles and aunts, who came for Sunday dinners and family reunions and funerals. A young person might ask just how Aunt Dorcas and Uncle Harvey are related to us, and no one could remember exactly how they came to be among us. But there they were and we loved them. They were family.

This will explain how my wife and I, who have no living brothers or sisters, happen to have a brother-in-law, David Lollis. Or, as we sometimes call him, our brother-in-law-in-law. (David married my wife's brother's widow.)

I have known David for a decade or a little longer and I keep learning new facts about his life and times. These days he runs an agency that funds low-cost housing for the poor, mostly in Appalachia. David spends much of his life on the road raising money.

Back in the sixties David escaped from Mississippi a little way ahead of some citizens concerned about his activities in regard to voting rights. "Communist" was the nicest thing they called him.

Just recently it came out that David had lived in New York for ten years and had taught at NYU. It was during that time that he and his friend Charlie were working with the cities of San Francisco and Oakland to help disadvantaged children. Every Tuesday David and

Charlie flew from New York to San Francisco, worked until Friday, and flew home.

Charlie was assigned to San Francisco and David to Oakland. Every night they would meet and talk about what they had done and make plans for the next day. David, a great fan of Jack London, had discovered a saloon on the Oakland waterfront where the author used to pass some time. It was little more than a shack, hanging over the bay. There was no electricity. Beer was kept in an icebox and kerosene lamps gave what little light there was.

Visitors pinned slips of paper with their names, or their business cards to the walls and ceiling, although those on the ceiling were soon blackened by soot from the lamps. David and Charlie left their cards in a corner where they held their meetings.

That was in 1969. Twenty-two years later David revisited the saloon, which, unlike neighboring buildings, had been bothered not at all by earthquakes. He sat in the very same corner; his card had disappeared, but Charlie's was there. Finding the card was a touching experience, for Charlie had recently died of cancer. Unable to keep his feelings to himself, David told his story to other customers, and they were moved, one of them recited a poem, and they all drank to Charlie.

It was, in fact, a sort of memorial service, a remembering before God one of his children who, in the words of the collect for the feast of St. Bernard of Clairvaux, "kindled with the flame of [God's] love, became a burning and shining light..." Ours is a society that seems increasingly more at home with Social Darwinism than with the holy requirements that we do justice, love kindness, and walk humbly with God.

Everybody changes the world just by being in it. Those who love the Lord change it for good, sometimes great changes, sometimes little ones. Most of us make little changes, but all—great deeds and small—open a place for the coming of the kingdom.

Some of us are called to heroic action. All of us are called to remember, to remind our children that there have been among us men and women who have shown us what it means to do justice and love kindness, and, like children themselves, to walk a while holding the hand of God.

The memory of him will not die but will live on from generation to generation; the nations will talk of his wisdom, and his praises will be sung in the assembly. If he lives long, he will leave a name in a thousand, and if he goes to his rest, his reputation is secure (Ecclesiasticus 39:9b-11 NEB).

I'll Be Talking
with You Later

Having lunch with Caden Blincoe was more than a quick meal; it was an occasion for communion. The first time Charlie Rice had lunch with Caden and me, Charlie was, among other things, interim editor of *Interchange* (the diocesan newspaper), a busy man. When the food was served he finished it quickly. I smiled to myself; Caden hadn't taken the first bite.

For Caden, our weekly lunch times were first for conversation, telling stories, doing show and tell. Food was important, but it was only an element. It was a rare noonday with Caden that I returned to Forward Movement's offices within an hour. Little by little I learned strategies to move things along when necessary. If I told a long story or if I excused myself for a few minutes, Caden ate. In the dozens of years of our lunches he ate more cold meals than I have in a lifetime.

We met in college, aspiring journalists. Our work took us on different paths for a number of years, but we met again as reporters for the *Lexington Leader*, now, alas, gone the way of many afternoon dailies. Caden was a fine reporter, and a craftsman writer. He polished his stories until they were gems. He worked with lead sentences until they were exactly what he wanted, words to get and hold the reader's attention.

His best pieces were about people. He got to know his subjects and did with words what a portraitist does with visual images. Caden met people easily and enjoyed making new friends. He has been described as having the demeanor of a Southern gentleman. He met people effortlessly and put them at ease at once. Caden seemed to be interested in everybody. He wanted to hear their stories and he wanted to tell his.

When he moved to Lexington it was some weeks before his wife Liz and their daughters Deborah and Sandy could join him. He disliked being alone and made occasion to be with people, one evening he showed up on my doorstep with two cans of chili and a bottle of tequila and said, "Let's have a Mexican party." Caden had the best qualities of Elwood P. Dowd in Mary Chase's play, "Harvey." If you said, "Let's get together," his response was, "When?"

Often we manned the newsroom on Saturday afternoons when little was going on. Caden sometimes amused himself—and the rest of us—by writing first sentences of novels—"He knew they were out there; he could hear them breathing."

He moved on to the Cincinnati *Enquirer* and I went to seminary and was called to a parish across the river in Covington. Then I moved away. When I began editing for Forward Movement Publications in the mid-eighties we began our weekly lunch meetings. By that time he had left the *Enquirer* and was a freelance writer.

For Caden, words were precious things, to be put together with thought and care. He enjoyed writing and reading, and championed the cause of literacy. He was the guiding spirit in forming an annual "out loud" festival in support of literacy. Writers read from their works, and participants included both established authors, such as the venerable James Still, and people who had just learned to read and write. The program has been adopted by Thomas More College and now bears Caden's name.

Among his favorite activities were the annual

storytelling festival in Jonesboro, Tennessee, and the cowboy poetry get-together in Elko, Nevada. He was always ready for new adventures. This year it would have been Alaska. Last year he signed up for a pilgrimage to Assisi led by Fr. Murray Bodo. There were twenty spots open and Caden got one of them. When the group gathered he found that he was the only non-Roman Catholic. The other nineteen were eighteen nuns and a monk. Before the trip was over he had taken part in Catholic services, including one in St. Peter's, Rome. I suspect he may have been the only Episcopal layman ever to do so.

Even before the trip to Italy Caden knew he was ill, and by the time he returned home he knew it was serious. Despite radical treatment that slowed the cancer's progress, he had but a year to live.

The last time I spoke to him he was in intensive care under heavy sedation and couldn't respond, but I know he heard me. I told him we still had a lot of stories to tell each other. Caden always ended our phone conversations with, "Well, I'll let you go now and I'll be talking with you later." I believe that's how it is. And what stories he will have to tell!

The Gospel
According to Badger

The Gospel according to Badger is somewhat shorter and simpler than John 3:16 or the Summary of the Law, but considering the age of the author, pretty comprehensive.

Badger (not his Christian name but, inexplicably, a nickname after a cat) is the four-year-old son of Deborah and John, friends of mine who live in a small town in New York. His parents are faithful Christians, the kind whose life asks this question, "Lord, how can we serve you?" They are also intelligent, educated, and artistic. But none of that quite explains the Gospel according to Badger, who was not yet three when he proclaimed it.

I have saved letters from his mother, knowing that sometime I would, with her permission, tell this story. When back in the middle of the summer a Sunday gospel reading from Matthew included the following words of Jesus, I figured the time had come: "I thank you, Father, Lord of heaven and earth, because you have hidden these things from the wise and the intelligent and have revealed them to infants . . ."

Excerpts from Deborah's letters tell the story:

"My son is an alert, intuitive boy. He will be three next month. Sometimes his sensitivities seem almost to go beyond what I would expect from what is available to his human senses—but of course, what else has he but human sensibilities, and so whatever he is perceiving is coming to him through them. What I am trying to say is that sometimes it seems to be as if he may be having some kind of direct experience of God—or, more specifically, Christ—which, because he does not have the intellectual baggage to cause him to question, comes to him with immediacy.

"We do not teach Badger about Christ or Jesus any more than we teach him about anything else in an active way. We make experiences and resources available to him, we live our lives in as close association as possible with him, and nature and Badger's own hunger for understanding do the rest. [Remember, Badger was not yet three.] Still, at Christmastime last year, the first when he was old enough to be intellectually able to grasp anything about the nativity, he was powerfully drawn to the images of the Jesus and the holy family. And he would spot images of the baby Jesus wherever he went, calling him by name.

"Recently Badger went through a period in which he mentioned two or three times that he would like to go to church. (He has been to churches in Santa Fe, and he had seen a movie in which there was an image of a cross on a tombstone—and he saw the cross and said, 'That church . . .')

"But the most amazing thing occurred this past Monday night when we attended the first meeting of the season of the fundamentalist Bible study in which we participated before Badger's birth. Despite the fact that we are far from being fundamentalists, or born-agains, or whatever, we find a genuine sense of Christian fellowship among these particular people, and a deep desire to find and follow a spiritual path. Not to be sneezed at, in our experience.

"Anyway, at a certain point in the evening, which was devoted to a study of the Book of Hebrews, Badger suddenly spoke up into a brief silence at the table—and what he had to say was not an echo of anything which had been said or read that night, or anything we have said to him. He spoke emphatically 'Jesus love me.' And there was a flurry of touched amazement at the table. And then he went on, softly, to say, 'Jesus love you,' as he pointed to each member of the study in turn. Finally he ended by saying, over and over, 'We love Jesus.' I still do not know what to make of it, except to wonder whether somehow Badger is in touch with a knowledge of the Christ which far surpasses my own."

From a letter received a few months later:

"You might be interested to know that Badger is anxious to be taken to church here in New York—that he requests to be taken to 'the big church' (whatever that means—in old time Appalachia, that meant the out of doors!), that he wants to take Sweetheart, his tiny teddy bear, so that Sweetheart can see the 'church'—by which, it turned out, he meant 'cross'. Seeing the cross . . . was given by Badger as being the reason he wanted to go to the church—this was discovered by us a few days after he had seen a crucifix in the hospital . . . and had asked to be reminded of what it was called. And he kept asking about the 'great big cross.' Perhaps he was remembering the Santuario de Chimayo [a shrine in New Mexico] where he visited a number of times . . . or perhaps he meant something else.

"It all feels very large and mysterious to me to hear my child urgently requesting all this. . . .

"But I am reminded now that Badger has made the connection between Christmas and Easter in his own direct and profound manner. When we were in New Mexico at Christmas time, Badger asked about the image of a crucifix, and we told him that the man was Jesus, and that Jesus loved everybody—and Badger knew about the baby Jesus. And he knew that Christmas was the day we celebrate the baby Jesus' birthday—and he asked to hold the crucifix that day, on Christmas Eve, so that he could sing birthday songs to the baby Jesus. Even as I write this, I get tears in my throat—the simplicity and beauty of that gift. We told him that we were sure that it made Jesus very happy."

Living in a world in which so much of what we do is based on transaction—deal-making,—it's hard even for dedicated Christians to resist trying to earn God's love. But there are no deals; Jesus invites us—even warns us—to come to him as little children did, readily and eagerly, without suspicion or guile.

Badger understands something that grownups have to learn and re-learn: the message of the cross, which so arrests his attention, is not "Be good or else," but "I love *you* and I love *you* and I love *you*. . . ."

Scott's Birthday Parade

Scott Peddie and I shared some interesting—and extraordinary—times. Once I stuck my toes in his mouth. Once there was a remarkable healing.

First the healing. Scott had major surgery; I don't now remember what for. There was a spot where the wound on his abdomen refused to close up. Quietly one day when we were at the Cathedral Domain, in the hills of Lee County, southeast of Lexington, he asked me to lay hands on him for healing. The two of us went into the huge old wooden Cathedral of St. George the Martyr and as Scott knelt at the rail, I laid hands on him for healing. And he was healed, right then, right there.

About the foot thing: For several—seemed like many—years we served together on the Commission on Ministry. That meant many, many nights sleeping in crowded quarters at the Domain. So crowded that sometimes the several bunks were a few inches apart.

I'm a "light sleeper" and I always prayed to get to sleep before the snorers started. There were always at least two in the cottage and Scott was one of them. I prayed, but Natural Law is firm: snorers always beat non-snorers in falling asleep. This time I had slept fitfully, awakened off and on through the night by snores. Sometime near daybreak Scott, whose bunk was next to mine, was frightening wildcats over the next ridge. I decided a gentle poke was appropriate, and because the weather was chilly I reached for his shoulder with my leg. I missed and stuck my toes in his open mouth.

Scott stopped snoring and opened his eyes. But I was quick and my leg was back under the cover and I pretended to be asleep. He never knew exactly what it was, but he always believed something unpleasant had happened just about dawn. I slept.

Scott was rector of St. Michael's before me. It was Scott who saw the church through its mission days into parishhood. Once, when I was still a layman, he tried to increase membership by recruiting my family from another parish. After St. Michael's, Scott served smaller parishes in Georgetown and Maysville before he retired.

At Commission on Ministry meetings Scott was our token curmudgeon, often asking pointed (and embarrassing) questions and making blunt (outrageous) statements not only to candidates for ordained ministry but, when he felt like it, to the bishop. Scott was a retired Air Force colonel and not given to pussyfooting or playing yes-man.

He knew, it seemed, hundreds of limericks and he was a good storyteller. Once when the commission met on Veterans' Day—November 11, formerly Armistice Day—he told us this one:

Scott grew up in a little town in Texas—Memphis, which he said was on the road to Dallas but didn't say where from. His father, an aviator, was the only soldier from Memphis to be killed in World War I, so his mother was the town's only Gold Star widow.

Scott was born on November 11, and every year when Memphis had its Armistice Day parade, there was little Scott, riding a float, the town's only Gold Star child, standing at attention, shouldering a little pop-gun, saluting, waving, having a wonderful time. This went on for a number of years. It wasn't until he was 12 that he realized the truth. This parade was not in celebration of his birthday. He was crushed.

Sometimes it takes quite a while and a jolting experience or two before we find out where we stand in the order of things. Where we think we are, or where we'd like to be, is usually at the center of creation, with all things made, if not by us, at least for us. My birthday. My toy. My bike. My house. My money. My church. My woman. My man. My honor. My team—if they win. My country. My world. My life.

Mine? Mine as long as I don't hug it to myself and squeeze the life out of it.

The world is ours to tend and care for, to love in, to enjoy—not to remake, fence, or keep. Trying to make our lives "mine" we lose all.

The parade isn't ours—mine—but we can be in it and enjoy it and ride the floats and salute and wave to the crowds, and that's a lot more fun than being the parade marshal and trying to get everybody in line and keeping them there and making sure it starts on time and worrying about cleaning up after the horses.

Jesus said we're not to worry about life, but to do it with everything we have. That's the way I remember Scott.

Not long into his retirement Scott died. I wrote a piece in the diocesan newspaper recalling his Armistice Day "birthday" parades. I hoped he knew that the solemn procession of his brothers and sisters in Christ on the day of his burial was at last the real thing; this was his grand and glorious birthday parade. This one was for him.

Seeing the Smile, Missing the Tear

The telephone rang late Saturday night. I grumbled, half asleep. My wife answered. A careless dialer, I thought. But Becky was listening and speaking quietly. Trouble. At last she whispered to me, "Bill killed himself."

Strangely, I slept well the rest of the night. It would be the last good sleep for awhile. Sunday morning I struggled celebrating the Holy Eucharist and preaching. Becky had gone to be with Bill's wife and their three boys. The youngest is our godson.

Monday night we drove to the town where Bill had been rector of the Episcopal church. Hundreds of people filed through the little nave to say a word or two to Colleen. On Tuesday Becky and I attended the memorial service for our friend.

For five years after seminary Bill had been the assistant in my parish. We worked well together. I tend to be a little introverted. Bill was outgoing, sociable. People were drawn to him. Everybody loved Bill. He was a great storyteller. He told about people back home in West Virginia, and he did all the voices and dialects; we laughed until we were sore.

He was a funny man; he made us laugh. Once when, at the end of a service, I had consumed all the remaining Sacrament, I turned the page to the postcommunion prayer to find that Bill had penciled in the words, "Burp here."

The homily at the memorial service was given by Bill's friend Michael Gatton, a Disciples of Christ minister. Dr. Gatton has been the public address announcer for high school football games, and he invited Bill, a former college player and avid football fan, to help him. In that town you can still get away with having a pre-game prayer. Once Dr. Gatton asked Bill to give the invocation. He handed the microphone to Bill and bowed his head. The next words he heard nearly gave him a stroke: "Dear Lord, please help us to beat their tails." Mercifully, Bill had turned the microphone off.

Bill was a funny man, always smiling. We saw his smile, but as Dr. Gatton said, we didn't see the tear in his eye. He hid it and that was deadly.

During the years we worked together I never had a clue that Bill was an alcoholic. The people in his parish didn't know until one Sunday morning he collapsed at the altar. The diocese and the parish supported him and he went away for intensive therapy. He returned apparently on top of his alcoholism.

He wasn't. He struggled over the past few years. He failed again and again. Finally he was separated from his family. Still he failed. But he went on smiling. About three weeks before his death I called him. He said everything was great. He had decided to teach full time at a community college and to be a supply priest on Sundays. He planned to work on a Ph.D. He would come and visit the next time he was in Lexington. But the next time I see Bill will be beyond this life.

For the twenty years we were friends, I missed the tear in his eye. He told funny stories, but inside he was fighting his demons.

Suicide is a terrible, terrible thing. If you have lived a moderate number of years probably you have been affected by someone close to you ending his life. Christians have been ambivalent about suicide. Is it the worst of sins, or the act of a person no longer in control?

Whatever the answer, there is an aura of spiritual oppressiveness, of evil, surrounding such a death. And the horror goes out in shock waves of pain and desolation, anger and grief, of disbelief and unbelief and hopelessness.

The second Sunday after Bill's death was harder; the lessons contained these words from Ecclesiastes: "It is an unhappy business that God has given to human beings to busy with. I saw all the deeds that are done under the sun; and see, all is vanity and a chasing after wind." Thank God the Bible doesn't end there but with books that tell of our Father's unrelenting love and limitless mercy and forgiveness.

I can't understand Bill's suicide, and I don't expect to. But I've taken from the events of that week a couple of reminders. First, don't try to fight your demons on your own. Remember that God gave us each other to care for each other, to help each other. The second is, be ready to help a struggling brother or sister. "Be kind, for everyone is fighting a hard battle."

A few days after Bill's death, the comic strip "For Better or Worse" had mother and daughter on a plane, headed home after a memorial service. Young Elizabeth says to her mother, "You're so quiet, Mom. Are you thinking about Grandma Marian?" "Yes," the mother says. "She was a kind person who led an interesting life. I was thinking that her memorial service was like the ending of a good novel." Elizabeth says, "I guess everyone's life is like a novel. Some of it is written by fate, some of it is written by God." "I agree," says the mother, "but the part we are ultimately judged by is the part we write ourselves."

On the Sunday when we read those depressing words from Ecclesiastes, we followed them with these from St. Paul: "As God's chosen ones, holy and beloved, clothe yourselves with compassion, kindness, humility, meekness, and patience. Bear with one another and, if anyone has a complaint against another, forgive each other; just as the Lord has forgiven you, so you must also forgive. Above all, clothe yourselves with love, which binds everything together in perfect harmony. And let the peace of Christ rule in your hearts, to which indeed you were called in the one body. And be thankful. Let the word of Christ dwell in you richly; teach and admonish one another in all wisdom; and with gratitude in your hearts sing psalms, hymns, and spiritual songs to God. And whatever you do, in words or deed, do everything in the name of the Lord Jesus, giving thanks to God the Father through him" (Col. 3:12-17).

Miracles Leaning
on Lampposts

The rosary before me on my desk is silver, the beads of its five decades smaller than BBs. Carol, a friend of many years, gave it to me when I was called to be rector of her parish. She said, smiling, "It's small enough to be used in a protestant church without anyone noticing."

Carol and her husband, Frank, were among the pioneers who established the congregation 25 years earlier in a school gymnasium. Now there were three Sunday morning services and devout wishes for a larger nave. She was the director of the parish pre-school. In my ten years as rector we had only one disagreement—what colors to use in the annual repainting of the classroom area. Carol always wanted green. I always wanted anything else. One year she let me win.

She was remarkable with the children. She never raised her voice and week after week in chapel I watched her get the attention of 80 children, quiet them and direct their actions with the movement of a finger and two or three spoken words. She had "presence."

Carol was also sick the last few years I was in the parish. Her breathing was bad and even the walk from her home to the church, a block away, was tiring. We worried about her, but she was composed and though she struggled with her health problems, she was as effective as always at the work she loved.

I had been gone three or four years when Carol died.

She slept poorly, and late one night, sitting at the kitchen table, Carol stopped breathing. Frank found her the next morning.

Two daughters and a son-in-law came to be with Frank. It was about 24 hours after Carol's death that the remarkable things happened. I tell the story as I received it. Frank, the younger daughter, Pam, and her husband, Charles, slept in upstairs bedrooms. The older daughter, Lucy, slept on the living room sofa. Sometime during the night—or very early morning—Lucy was awakened by sounds from the kitchen. Assuming another family member was sleepless, Lucy went into the kitchen. Her mother was there. Lucy was surprised but not frightened. They sat together at the table and talked. Carol looked renewed, healthy. She comforted her daughter and told her how wonderful her new life was. Lucy wanted to know what it was like. Carol told her to close her eyes and she would see. Lucy saw—she had no words to tell what it was like—an indescribably beautiful "landscape" whose light came not from an outside source but from within. She no longer saw her mother but, to use her word, "aspects" of her mother.

And then Carol and the vision were gone.

Frank was the first one down in the morning. Before Lucy could tell him what had happened, Frank poured out the story of how he had awakened in the morning to a bright light in the bedroom and Carol's voice giving him words of comfort.

While Lucy and Frank marveled at their experience, Pam came downstairs with a similar story and was followed shortly by Charles who had also been visited by Carol. Each person in the household had, individually, met Carol, and through her words and presence been given reassurance and peace.

About a year later I had lunch with Frank. He missed Carol very much, but the extraordinary happenings following her death had changed him. He was at peace and I had a sense that he was patiently waiting. He died, as I remember, within a few months of our meeting.

In his book, *Ring of Truth*, J.B. Philips, author of *Your God is Too Small* and translator of *The New Testament in Modern English*, recounts this experience: Philips had seen C.S. Lewis in person only once but had corresponded with him a fair amount. A few days after Lewis's death in 1963, while Philips was watching TV, Lewis "appeared" sitting in a chair near Philips. Lewis glowed with good health, grinned broadly, and said a few words "which were particularly relevant to the difficult circumstances" through which Philips was passing. Philips wrote that he had not been thinking about Lewis. He was not alarmed nor surprised by the visitation. A week later Lewis appeared, "Even more rosily radiant than before, and repeated to me the same message, which was very important to me at the time."

Philips sought the counsel of a "certain saintly bishop" who, unsurprised, told him "this sort of thing is happening all the time."

And, indeed, apparently it is. Unsure whether or how to write the story about Carol, I consulted a trusted friend who urged me to do it, and then told me of hearing plainly the voice of a departed loved one give a message she needed to hear. I know of other persons' experiences, and realize that some people explain them away as hallucinations—as well some may be.

But characterizing as hallucination the events in the home of Carol and Frank, involving four people individually, would be pushing that explanation further than I am willing to go. Perhaps we don't tell each other about such experiences because they are so personal. Or maybe we would be embarrassed to talk of the supernatural in a society that is turned in upon itself and has no room for miracles.

Too bad.

Years ago I sat in a classroom listening to Dr. Elisabeth

Kubler-Ross, one of the world's best known psychiatrists, tell about meeting a patient who had died. The class was made up of professionals—many nurses and ministers; some other people. In the middle of this story they kept interrupting, asking all kinds of questions that had nothing to do with what the doctor was saying. At least one class member rose to her feet and said, in effect, "Are you all nuts? Elisabeth is telling us about talking with a dead woman and you're asking about hospital administration. Can't you hear what she's saying?"

That experience reminds me of a scene in Mary Chase's play, "Harvey." The psychiatrist has become convinced, against everything he believed, that there really is a six-foot invisible rabbit. "Fly-specs," he says, "I've been spending my life among fly-specs while miracles have been leaning on lampposts on 18th and Fairfax."

Just so.

Comes UPS

Time, like an ever-rolling stream, bears all our years away . . .
(680, Hymnal 1982).

The deacon from the little church in Eastern Kentucky called to tell me that my friend Perry had died. The last time Perry and I had talked by telephone his words were almost unintelligible, and about the only thing I understood was, "I want you to say the words over me."

His cancer had been discovered almost two years before, and there were times when the disease seemed to be winning and times when Perry, his wife Betty, and the doctor seemed to be winning. It appeared the cancer won at last, but that was illusory.

Characteristically, at the end Perry gave us a couple of good laughs to balance our tears.

The memorial service was held in the Presbyterian church because the Episcopal church wasn't big enough. As we stood in the entranceway watching the crowd grow to standing-room-size-only, his wife, Betty, said to me, "He would have hated this." "Yes," I said, "let's do it."

He would have "hated this" because it was a lot of fuss. Perry was a thoughtful, practical man, a devout man, and wonderfully, dryly humorous. While he might amusedly grumble about all the trouble we were going to, he would have been thankful for our loving presence. And perhaps he was.

The deacon called me on a Wednesday and said the memorial service probably would be the following

Tuesday. That seemed a long time. It seemed a long time to Betty, too. Even though the cremation must be done in a city some distance away, should it take a week to return the ashes? Betty kept asking why and at last the deacon confessed. Secretly, Perry had given him instructions that instead of having the funeral home return his ashes at a charge of $200, they should be shipped UPS for $20. When the deacon tried to argue with him, Perry, with great difficulty managed these words: "Put a stamp on me!"

It was just the sort of practical thing Perry would do. He had spent much of his time and his limited energy over the past two years making arrangements so his family would be financially secure. He also had focused on his relationship with God, and Perry and I met from time to time when he was in the city for treatments.

We talked a good deal about spiritual exercises, especially forms of meditation. One he often used I had picked up years ago in Tucson in a seminar on Native American medicine. There is a good deal of imaging, ending with an exercise involving a little black stone called an "Apache Tear." (I forget the scientific name.) In a prayerful, sacramental gesture, one puts into the stone all that is harmful—sins, worries, fears, despair—and then in the imagination places the stone in a stream or in the surf so God can wash away all that burdens the soul. The stone is retrieved and kept for another time.

Near the end of his life Perry was upset because he couldn't find the Apache Tear. "Maybe it all washed away, Dad," his son suggested.

When Perry's ashes were at last returned, the boy saved a little to take to the beach his father loved. Sometime soon the ashes, too, will be washed away. Time, like an ever-rolling stream, will bear away our years as well as all stones and ashes and the streams and beaches and our best and worst deeds and the memory of it all. But that's not the end of the story; the end of the story for Perry, and for us, is this:

The earth and the heavens will perish, but God will endure; they all will wear out, but God's years will never end, and his beloved children, safe in him, will live to remember "When the stars were an old tale."

Mary's Cross

Truly I tell you, just as you did it to one of the least of these who are members of my family, you did it to me (Matthew 25:40).

Mary places two items on the kitchen table at St. Agnes House. One is a framed photograph. The other is a gold cross. We are having coffee after the morning Eucharist in the chapel. First she shows a picture of her father, the Rev. Robert C. Kilbourn, holding the infant Mary beside a baptismal font.

Mary Kilbourn-Huey, deacon and nurse, says she was a daddy's girl. She was interested in what he did and often accompanied him on his calls when he was rector of the Church of the Nativity in Maysville, Kentucky, just across the Ohio River from Aberdeen. When homeless people came to the rectory door for help, they were invited to eat with the family. If they chose to have their food outside, Mary sometimes sat with them. In the years before women were ordained, Mary and her mother—another Mary among a slew of Marys in *her* life (Mary Esther, Mary Frances, Mary Jo and two Mary Elizabeths)—worked like Marthas in the church.

Now Mary hands me the gold cross. I've seen it before but I wanted to examine it closely. The cross is about two and a half inches high, on a chain. Her father's parents gave it to him on the Easter following his ordination as a deacon. The inscriptions are "R.C.K." and "Easter 1941." A closer look reveals a number of indentations in the cross. Mary explains that she, her sister and her two brothers teethed on the cross as their father held them in his arms.

Fr. Kilbourn died of a heart attack in 1972, but Maysville continued to be home for the Kilbourns, and even now, living miles away in a city, when Mary speaks of the old river town, there is a hint of longing in her voice.

St. Agnes House sits on a quiet cul-de-sac near a university and a seminary. Mary studied at both institutions and at a school of nursing a couple of blocks away. Episcopalians established St. Agnes House more than two decades ago as a place where out-of-town cancer patients and their families could stay during outpatient treatment at the university's medical center. There are 11 bedrooms, two kitchens and common areas available for residents, but more important, there is hospitality and companionship.

For half its life St. Agnes House was staffed by sisters of the Society of St. Margaret. Mary is the second manager since the sisters left. She and her husband, Terry, live in an apartment on the second floor, along with Mary's mother. Despite the help of many volunteers, managing means doing a hundred things every day, every night; time off is minimal.

Little miracles happen. A man who hasn't been in a church for ten years begins attending the daily Eucharist. He stays through the Peace, then leaves. Once a week, patients and their families come to the chapel foi informal sessions of hymn singing and story telling. One day in the garden a patient asks Mary when they're going to sing again. She says, "Right now," fetches her dulcimer and returns to play music with him.

Nearly all the residents are from rural, predominantly protestant areas, and there is no proselytizing. Still, four persons have been baptized in the chapel and others baptized back in their hometowns after spending time at St. Agnes House.

It would make a good story if I could write that, cutting her teeth on the cross brought Mary to this holy work. In a sense that's true, but I go back to the first object she showed me—the photo of the child at the baptismal font. This is where we all begin. Then, at some point we make the first of countless choices in which we will remember, or not, that we have been washed in eternal waters, marked with the sign of the cross and made Christ's own forever. We can say this; that the small cross was one of the first things Mary saw and touched in her life and who knows what memories of it her soul stored, influencing the choices that have kept her near the original.

Deep Calls Unto Deep

For more years now than I can count, some time, some place, I go to the sea.

Since I don't swim in it and never come back with a tan, friends have always asked, "What for?"

I go there to recover my perspective, to recover my health, to recover my sanity. I go to the ocean to find peace, to embrace life, to rediscover myself. The ocean is clean—or it looks clean. It's salty and the salt is cleansing, preserving. And the wind, blowing in over the water disperses a mental smog in which my thoughts have been wandering, finding it hard to breathe, hard to see.

Other people don't have to go to the ocean to be renewed. Some do it in the mountains or in a monastery or at Opryland or even in the living room in front of the TV. Maybe I could find renewal in those places, but I know I find it at the ocean, so I go there.

I make a great effort not to think. It's wonderful. I learn so much more by seeing, listening, letting my sense teach me things, letting God's voice be heard where there is usually babble.

One night I walked out to the end of our boardwalk at Holden Beach, N.C. I stood on the dune, looking down at the surf of the incoming tide. The sky in the east was already dark and the water was a deep gray, the white edge of the rollers the only contrast.

I thought of the psalmist's words, "Deep calls unto deep." The deep of the sea called that night to the deep in me. The life of the sea spoke to the life in me. The power of the sea awakened awe in me. The movement of the sea described the eternity God had set in my heart. The darkness of the sea searched the shadowy places of my soul. The hidden life of the sea promised life still unawakened in me.

The loneliness of the sea called to the loneliness in me, the loneliness of mankind, an aloneness made of secrets, of questions, of fears, of lusts, of longings, of homesickness. A solitude reaching back to Eden, separating man from God and man from man.

I was alone on the dune, watching the darkening sea, listening as deep called unto deep. Then, I looked away down the strand, and there, against the pale rose of the last light of the world, I saw the silhouette of another man, watching the sea, and I wondered what his thoughts were, and then I knew that for him, too, deep called unto deep, and though I might never meet him, I was comforted to know that this night, he there, and I here, watched and listened. He was a brother.

Deep calls unto deep.

Holden Beach is an island, cut off from the mainland by the intercoastal waterway. There is a strand eight miles long, and hundreds of cottages sit along the beach. Across narrow inlets to the east and west are Long Beach and Ocean Isle. There is a string of these islands, all much the same, beach house after beach house for miles and miles along the coast of Brunswick County.

I know a lot of people in those houses. Some are from former parishes of mine, some from other towns in Kentucky. There are all kinds, colors, and sorts of people here. There are doctors and merchants and teenagers on vacation. There are teachers and musicians and people who have retired. There are some who have come to make a buck off the tourists. There are shop clerks and financiers. There are rich people and poor people, and week after week they come to live—to play and read and swim and rest—and to watch and listen by the sea.

In meditations in which I imagine meetings with Jesus, the scene is the seaside, and over the years it has come to be obvious that the sea is, in those meditations, a symbol of God. As I've talked with people about this I've found that for many of them, too, the sea is in some way associated with God. They may not be able to articulate it, but the connection is there.

Why do we live along the strand? Because deep calls unto deep and for some of us this is where that call brings us. There we stand in the twilight watching, listening, knowing that even here at the edge of the world, there is a Deep beyond this vast deep that calls to us. This far have we come, and no further can we go. Not yet.

Paul wrote, "Let your thoughts be on heavenly things, not on the things that are on the earth, because you have died, and now the life you have is hidden with Christ in God. But when Christ is revealed—and he is your life— you too will be revealed in all your glory with him" (Colossians 3:2-4).

That's why we're at the beach, or on a mountaintop, or in a monastic cell—Greek and Jew, circumcised and uncircumcised, barbarian and Scythian, slave and free— why sometimes, no matter where we are, we just stop and watch and listen as deep calls unto deep. The heart of God calls to the heart of man.

We come to the edge of the world knowing in our hearts there is something more, something indescribable, some truth almost remembered, unutterable, and that truth is that our life is hidden with Christ in God and we're waiting in the solitude of paradise lost for that life to be revealed in all its glory.

Not yet, but someday, someday . . .

Becky's Leaf

A few weeks ago Becky sat next to my step-daughter and across from my wife and me at a neighborhood restaurant. It was a good-bye meal in Becky's honor. She was about to undertake the first step in her plan to earn graduate degrees in Ivy League country. Not surprisingly—this was Becky, after all—she was starting out in Colorado. Don't ask.

Becky, 24, is a rare person. Despite her being closer to my step-daughter's age and similarly eclectic in manner of dress, and despite other differences among us in our tastes, our political, social and theological views, she is a friend of all three of us. During dinner we talked about Joseph Campbell, massage therapy, non-alcoholic beer, her family, clothes, Jesus, the barbecue, Rush Limbaugh, the waiter my step-daughter found attractive, graduate courses, ACTs, SATs, GREs, the dessert menu. Among other things.

Becky is a Christian pilgrim. She has been following Jesus, working along the way, looking for signs of her vocation. She has, she believes, come upon them.

I have known her and her mother for a long time. (In high school I was once in love with Becky's aunt-to-be.) I see her now as an adult and not as a grown-up version of the child I first met, and I am surprised and then delighted when she recalls an incident from that time years ago.

It was a fall day, much like the one on which I write this, late in the afternoon. I had stopped to talk with

Becky's mother. It had been a long, tiring day. As I walked to my car, a small person met me, reached up, and handed me a leaf. It was to me a wonderful act of kindness and grace, and in the strength of it I went on to finish my day's work. I put the leaf in my Prayer Book.

In the days they spent together before Becky's departure, her mother had recalled the day and also remembered that I had told of the gift in a sermon, naming the giver a "cheerful giver."

I am a "keeper" and have copies of pretty much every sermon I have ever written. Once—no, twice—I organized them. Maybe three times. But picking out one here and there I have unorganized them into several leaning piles. Nevertheless, I began searching with some confidence for the piece about Becky and the leaf, but as days passed hope of immediate discovery failed.

I was a little disappointed not to find it now, but guess what I did find: the leaf, still in the now-retired Prayer Book, still holding much of the color of that afternoon, affirming Jesus' insistence on paying attention to children and learning from them.

Catherine Miles Wallace wrote: "Once, when I had the flu, a kid barely able to walk covered my shoulders with a prized blanket that she still has on the foot of her bed more than a decade later. She patted my head and crooned softly, then tottered away . . .

"Generosity is in fact deeply seated within us and just as profoundly repressed by the ordinary callous interchange of adult life. Babies don't offer you a swig from their bottles because they think you are thirsty, or to prove they are one-up in this apple juice business, or to alleviate their guilt at consuming such an enormous percentage of the earth's resources."

They do it, she wrote, because giving is natural and children live in the present moment; adults learn to plan and think ahead and calculate and miss much of the joy of living now.

Sometime, when I'm looking for something else, I'll find that sermon. Today it doesn't matter because the story is pressed between the pages of the Prayer Book and calls up a memory as present and golden as this October afternoon.

Tale of Two Sisters

I'll call them Hallie and Lois, sisters. Hallie I know very well, Lois hardly at all.

They were the only children of a fairly well-to-do family. They were bright and strong-willed. Like many siblings, they squabbled, but the squabbling continued into adulthood.

Hallie was quicker of wit and sharper of tongue, and in their disagreements Lois always got the worst of it. So Lois nursed her hurts, and her grudge against her sister grew and grew.

It may have been because Lois was overmatched in this feud that their mother seemed to favor her. That made Hallie mad; and, I think, though she would never have said it this way, she felt, "Mother always liked you better."

Hallie was older. She went off to college and fell in love with learning and with the academic life in general. She decided she would teach. She was a brilliant student and went from success to success, earning her Ph. D. and becoming a professor in a prestigious program.

Lois never went so far. She married before she finished college and, in Hallie's opinion, married beneath her. Hallie had married a scholar.

Lois married a "working man" who sometimes had no job.

The sisters lived apart for years, but then circumstances brought them and their families to live near each other. Hallie and her husband had one child, born as

Hallie approached middle age. Lois was mother of two or three.

The bickering was renewed. Lois, I think, was jealous of Hallie's success. Hallie was jealous of her mother's protectiveness of her sister. Their mother's death did not end the warfare.

Years passed. Hallie raised an ungrateful, hateful child. And she and her unfaithful husband were divorced. She had cancer and, with surgery and chemotherapy, she survived it.

A long time afterward, during a routine physical examination, the doctor found some suspicious signs. Tests showed that Hallie's body was riddled with cancer. To everyone's surprise, her long-estranged son returned for a while to help her. The chemotherapy made Hallie terribly weak and horribly sick. She could not care for herself.

Then one day Lois came. She said, "Hallie, all that enmity, all that jealousy, all that hatred, all those terrible words, are in the past. It's over." And she began to care for Hallie, taking her for treatments, helping her walk, being with her when she was sick, cleaning up the messes.

There is one image from their story that stays with me. Hallie was sick and in pain, her strength and her will near exhaustion. Lois, worn out herself, lay down on the bed beside her sister and began to rub her back. It was all she could think of to do. And it was helpful. She rubbed and rubbed, and finally, weary, she fell asleep beside her sister.

Hallie told me about that. She may not survive this sickness, but she and Lois have been healed.

God shows up unexpectedly, in unexpected places, and in unexpected people. You can always tell when God is in a situation.

Wherever love is, there is God. There is no love without God; there is no God without love. All love comes through the Cross. Love burst forth two millennia ago like the Big Bang, across and through all dimensions of existence.

Love brings reconciliation where there is separation. Love brings wholeness where something is damaged. Love brings peace, harmony, where there is chaos.

Love, said St. Paul, is patient, kind, never envious, boastful, arrogant or rude. Love doesn't insist on its own way. It's not irritable or resentful, doesn't rejoice in wrongdoing, but rejoices in truth. Love bears all things, believes all things, hopes all things, endures all things.

And best of all, Love never ends, never gives up. In spite of our enmity to him and to each other, God comes himself to be with us, to clean up our messes, and to lie down with us in our dying to give us life.

Libby and Bud

This is a little story about love.

An early heart attack got Bud's attention. When he was released from the hospital he began coming to church with his teen-age nephew, an acolyte in my first parish. I baptized Bud and the church became the center of his life.

He was a mail carrier. He shared a house with his older brother, also a bachelor. Bud was by nature a quiet and reflective man, and after the heart attack he thought a lot about his solitary life; his brother was such a different kind of person that he offered little company. Bud thought about his mortality. When the 17-year locust came he told me he didn't expect to see them return. In fact, he was around when they reappeared, and the reason, I believe with all my heart, was Libby.

Libby was a widow, somewhere in her sixties—young and vital sixties—several years older than Bud. Invited by a neighbor, she began coming to church and she and Bud became friends. After a few months they became a couple, and at most church gatherings—we had a lot of them—they arrived together and left together.

It was a happy meeting; Libby and Bud clearly loved each other and people began to whisper and smile about a wedding. When Bud's brother died, expectations in that little congregation rose sharply. Months passed and I moved to another assignment and there had been no wedding.

In the years that followed I saw Libby and Bud at

church conventions and on other occasions that brought me back to their parish. They continued to be happily, comfortably, contentedly in love. On the 20th anniversary of my ordination to the priesthood I was nearby and invited to celebrate the Eucharist in my former church. I had been gone for 16 years and was surprised and delighted when numbers of old friends came to the service and invited me to a party in the parish house afterward.

When I had greeted and talked with everyone else I sat down by Bud. I don't remember the conversation that led up to it, but after awhile Bud was quietly reciting a poem he had composed about his meeting with Libby and their love for each other. When I could bring myself to speak I asked for a copy of the poem and Bud said he would send it. Maybe because his health began to fail, or maybe because the words were too private to put in writing, Bud, always generous and dependable, never produced the copy.

I next saw him a year later at his house. Libby was with him that day, caring for him. The three of us knew he was dying. I gave him communion and anointed him. A couple of weeks later his nephew called to tell me Bud was dead. I returned to read the burial office.

Libby lived for a few more years, and when I last visited her she was still agelessly beautiful. She talked of heaven and what it would be like and whom she would meet on her dying day.

Looking back at Libby and Bud's life together, I discern a third Presence. I now believe that on the night of my anniversary Bud was telling me about the three of them. Maybe it's just as well the words he said aren't written anywhere. I suspect their effect, their meaning, had a lot to do with Bud's saying them. As Malcolm Muggeridge said about Luke's account of the Emmaus Road encounter, "There was something in the very language and manner of it which breathed truth."

There was never a wedding but there was such a strong joining of souls that I am in awe at the memory of it and certain that it goes on somewhere beyond time and space. Some of us are called to marriage, some are not; all of us are called to love. Paul wrote, "The last enemy to be destroyed is death." Love is stronger than death, outlasts death. And as surely as love is stronger than the last enemy, love is stronger than the next-to-last enemy, loneliness.

Ernest Sticks to It

A few weeks ago, Paige, a young woman friend of ours, went with her boyfriend, Harry, for an eye examination. While they were waiting, a middle-aged man emerged from the examining rooms and asked the receptionist to call a taxi to take him to the Hope Center. The Hope Center is a wonderful institution that ministers to the homeless and to others in trouble, most of whom have little hope left—many recovering from alcoholism or drug addiction. The receptionist said she was too busy to call a cab.

Paige overheard and told the man that if he could wait until Harry was finished, they would take him to the Hope Center. Members of Paige's family have served as volunteers there and know its good work. The man—his name was Ernest—said he didn't want to be a bother, but Paige persuaded him. She is the kind of lady it's hard to say no to.

In the car, Paige asked Ernest where he was from. Shelby County, he said.

"Really, do you know my Uncle Gene?"

"I sure do. I work for him sometimes."

Ernest comes from a village near the place where Paige's mother, Carolyn, and her stepfather, Guy, grew up. Ernest's mother-in-law, Eva, had been housekeeper for Guy's family. Guy told me later that she had been a second mother to him; he had gone to see her not long ago. Eva's husband had been a truck driver for Guy's father.

Ernest is the only son of a Baptist minister—his

mother. He has four sisters, all college graduates and successful. He has children himself.

Ernest's story is not unusual. He abused drugs and alcohol for 20 years. When he got into some relatively minor trouble with the law and faced three to six months in jail, his lawyer asked if he wanted to be rid of his addiction. He did. The lawyer requested that the judge send Ernest to the Hope Center. When Paige met him he had been there a little more than a month, with five to go.

It's not an easy program: zero tolerance for those who don't stick to it. Ernest was sticking to it. He had his Alcoholics Anonymous 30-day chip, but he told Paige he needed a sponsor. Paige said, "Pops will be your sponsor," volunteering her step-father, Guy, a recovering alcoholic. Guy was glad to help. He called Ernest and the next Sunday took him and two other men from the center to an AA meeting. Afterward, Guy invited all of them home for a meal.

Ernest asked to say the blessing.

Guy is a good friend and when I asked about this undertaking he said, "I'm only doing for him what was done for me."

While it's true that Guy is doing for Ernest what was done for him—he had a sponsor years ago—I know he is moved by something deeper than mere duty. Helping Ernest is an act of love by a man with a good heart.

There seems to me some connection between the story of Guy and Ernest, their experiences, where they came from historically, geographically, economically, and Paul's letter to Philemon, the only one of the apostle's personal letters we have. In it Paul called in a favor. He asked Philemon to take back a runaway slave, Onesimus—and to take him back not as a slave but as a Christian brother. Life "in Christ"—Paul's wonderful expression—breaks down the usual barriers between people: class, culture and race.

Being a Christian changes us; all our relationships are altered. For those in Christ, caring, kindness, service are a way of life—*the* way of life. Differences by which the world orders itself don't matter—employee/employer, servant/master, weak/strong, those who are down/those who are up. Those who can help serve those who need help.

We all know at least something of what it means to be "in Christ," and every time we do a kindness, it is as if we are echoing Guy's modest disclaimer, "I'm only doing for her or him what was done for me—by the Lord Christ."

Phil Learns He Is a Jew

When my wife Becky and I visited our friends Phil and Ann Thomas in New Orleans, we stayed in the city except for one night spent at their house on Irish Bayou. Phil grew up with water and boats and is uncomfortable if he spends too much time on dry land.

One day, Ann told us, Phil was fishing off their dock and an alligator took his line, pulled and broke it. The hook was set, and they watched as the bobber on the line moved away into the bayou. A little while later, while trying to do something he is too old to do, Phil fell in the water. He was okay, but having a hard time climbing out . . . until Ann spotted the bobber moving quickly toward the dock and shouted warning. It's surprising how fast a 250-pound man on Medicare can, under certain circumstances, lift himself up.

After last Christmas Phil and Ann Thomas visited us for a couple of days. Phil was a seminary classmate, my best friend in seminary, best man when Becky and I married. He is retired from active priesthood and he and Ann have a bed and breakfast across the street from Commander's Palace in the Garden District of New Orleans, two blocks from the St. Charles Street trolley.

Their son John lives in Brevard, North Carolina. He is married to a lovely lady and they have three little daughters. Although John's wife is Jewish and practices her faith, she and the girls often attend St. Philip's Church with John.

Not long ago Phil was talking with one of the children,

who didn't know her grandfather was a priest. She mentioned church. Phil said, "You go to church?" "Yes." "Where do you go to church?" "We go to St. Philip's where all the Jewish people go." "Really! Do you know any Jewish people?" "Sure, I'm Jewish and Mama is Jewish and my sisters are Jewish." "What about Papa?" "No, Papa does go to St. Philip's, but he's an Episcopalian."

Well, we've been pressing the idea of inclusiveness in the Episcopal Church for years.

The world, the mix of peoples and faiths, has really changed. Or has it? A few days after Phil told me that story I came across this prayer from the *Oxford Book of Prayer:*

"Almighty God, as your Son our Savior was born of a Hebrew mother, but rejoiced in the faith of a Syrian woman and of a Roman soldier, welcomed the Greeks who sought him, and suffered a man from Africa to carry his cross, so teach us to regard all faithful people as fellow heirs of the kingdom of Jesus Christ."

Phil told me another story. When his grandmother died, and the family went to her home to pack things up, to clear things out, they found under her mattress her prayer book. A Jewish prayer book. The fact that she was Jewish was unknown to his generation. In his grandmother's time and in the place where the family lived, it was better to be a Christian. But she never let go of her heritage, and Phil keeps her prayer book as a treasure of the heart. Because you are a Jew or not through your mother's line, Phil the priest with the Jewish grandchildren learned that he, too, is technically, by birth, a Jew.

Now, the point of all that is not to say that all religions are valid or the same and it doesn't matter what you believe. But we are all human beings, created by God, loved by God. And I believe that God honors as faithfulness all our true and honest attempts to find him, to know him.

Evelyn Underhill wrote: "Christ is a Light to lighten the Gentiles as the Glory of his people Israel. Think of what the Gentile was when these words were written— an absolute outsider. All cozy religious exclusiveness falls before that thought . . . all are called and welcomed and accepted. Our own adoration and deep certitude, if God in his mercy gives us that, is never to break our brother-hood with those who come longer journeys by other paths, led by a different star. The Magi took more trouble than the shepherds. The intellectual virtues and intellec-tual longings of men are all blessed by Christ."

Christ is Lord of all humankind. Whether they know it or not, whether they immediately recognize him or not. Everybody is welcome, everybody is invited into the kingdom. Everybody is invited by this extraordinary person, Jesus, Son of Man, Son of God, who promised, "And I, when I am lifted up from the earth, will draw all people to myself."

What a Foolish Woman!

David, my brother-in-law, is a good man. His father, a Disciples of Christ minister, passed on his social conscience to his son. David has worked all his adult life in government and private agencies to help make life better for the poor and the oppressed in our society.

He is now the executive officer for an organization that helps people with lower incomes buy homes. His duties, which include raising money, keep him traveling, mostly by car. David can put 100,000 miles on a Honda between Thanksgiving and Christmas—well, maybe Epiphany.

A peculiarity is that he resists stopping for gas until it's almost too late. His wife Betty says he burns out the low fuel warning lights on his cars. Inevitably, sometimes he miscalculates.

Two stories:

Once in a southeastern Kentucky town, David had so little gas left in the tank that when he parked on a slope the fuel pump couldn't get to the dregs. He walked to a nearby filling station and told the attendant his problem. Could he borrow a can to carry gas back to his car?

"Well," the woman said, "I'd let you borrow it, but somebody took it and didn't bring it back." He walked to a second station. No cans there. At last, after about a mile, he came to a hardware store and bought a can. He carried it back to the first filling station to fill it up.

"Oh," said the attendant, "I didn't know you wanted to buy a can. I've got plenty for sale."

A couple of weeks ago David was on the interstate between Charleston and Morgantown, West Virginia. He usually knows how low his gas is by watching the odometer. But this time he hadn't calculated that it's uphill to Morgantown, and besides, he was late and going faster than usual. And so, just five miles short of his goal, the car spit a couple of times and died. It expired, fortunately, just at an exit, and David coasted onto the off-ramp. There were no gas stations, no businesses at all at the interchange.

He hadn't been sitting there more than a couple of minutes when a pick-up truck stopped, and a woman asked if he needed help. He told her his problem. She said he could borrow a can at her daddy's farm down the road.

She would drive him up the interstate to get gas and bring him back. Amazed that a woman, by herself, offered this help, David climbed into the cab, and they drove to the farm. The woman left him in the truck while she went to the barn. "You're in luck," she said when she returned, carrying a five-gallon can. "It's full of gas."

She drove him back to his car. David put the gas in the Honda, offered effusive thanks, and pulled out a $20 bill to pay for the gas and the help. No, the woman said, "Sometime you can stop and help me when I'm in the same fix."

"But I'm not likely ever to come across you out of gas on the side of the road," David answered.

"Well," the woman said, "then do it for somebody else."

And she drove away.

What a foolish woman! I don't know anybody who picks up strangers. Maybe in some parts of the country it's not unusual. But driving in cities, as I do, I am conscious of whether my car doors are locked, and there are neighborhoods where I'm not likely to roll down my window more than a couple of inches if a stranger approaches to speak to me.

What a foolish woman! David might have been a madman, an escaping bank robber, a serial killer. He doesn't look like any of those, but often they don't either.

Foolishness is, like beauty, in the eye of the beholder. Or, not so much in the eye as in the mind and heart and will.

There is a foolishness of the world and there is the foolishness of God.

In a Sunday collect we pray for God to increase his foolishness among us. [St. Paul wrote that the wisdom of this world is foolishness to God (1 Cor 3:19).] God's gifts of faith, hope and charity, none of which fits in with being secure or getting ahead in the world. We pray to love what God commands so that we might obtain what he promises.

I love the flow of the words and the phrasing of that collect, but when I think of the woman in West Virginia, I'm reminded that loving what God commands, and carrying around the gifts of faith, hope and charity is a tough business. It takes courage and even daring. It requires a certain amount of foolishness.

St. Paul, who knew something about foolishness, wrote "We are treated as imposters, and yet are true; as unknown, and yet well known; as dying, and behold we live; as punished, and yet not killed; as sorrowful, yet always rejoicing, as poor, yet making many rich; as having nothing, and yet possessing everything" (2 Corinthians 6:4ff).

Once in his travels, Jesus was hailed by a blind man named Bartimaeus. Jesus stopped and they brought Bartimaeus to him. Jesus said, "What do you want me to do for you?" Bartimaeus knew exactly what he wanted;

he said, "Master, let me receive my sight." And he received his sight and followed Jesus.

I'm struck by Jesus' question, "What do you want me to do for you?" Bartimaeus' answer was ready; no hemming and hawing as if he had been offered three wishes by a genie. Jesus' question is eternally posed to us—each of us and all of us as the Church.

There are at least two considerations in answering: One is that we have an answer that we've thought through; our answer, our prayer can't be just a matter of form. It's a serious question—a really serious question— and it demands a serious answer. The second consideration is that we be ready to receive what we ask for, to treat it as the precious gift it is, and to use it generously, graciously, courageously, lovingly and maybe even foolishly—following Jesus.

Could Have Been
an Angel

Every year during Advent my wife Becky and I watch again a few old movies. Becky's favorite is "Pocketful of Miracles." Mine is "The Bishop's Wife" in which Cary Grant plays an angel sent in answer to the bishop's prayer for help in building a new cathedral. The bishop gets help in learning what's really important. And along the way the angel helps a number of other people—stopping a baby carriage from rolling in front of a car, giving an aged professor a tidbit of information to get him started on writing his long-talked about and longer-postponed book, creating an ever-full bottle of sherry that cheers but does not inebriate. When the angel has done all he can do, he leaves, and although everyone's life is changed, no one can remember that he was ever present. How many times might angels have interceded in our lives and we have either forgotten or didn't recognize them? Hmmm.

Which, of course, brings me to a story. A year or more ago my son Robert and daughter-in-law Donna were spending a weekend across the Ohio in Augusta, Kentucky. In an art gallery Donna was looking at some pictures of England's Bronte country and got into a conversation with the English proprietor, Barbara. How had she found her way to this little river town in Northern Kentucky?

Years ago a young teacher from Cincinnati—I don't know his name and will call him Joe—came to live for awhile in her town in England. Barbara's family befriended him, sort of adopted him. After his work was finished he returned to the United States and afterward visited the English family only once. Although they felt close to Joe, they somehow lost touch.

It was perhaps twenty years later—Donna couldn't remember—that Barbara, now a teacher with grown children, and a widow, was giving a guided tour in a cathedral. Usually, she said, she didn't talk much with American tourists, but one day she asked a visitor where he was from and he said, "Cincinnati." She said, "I know someone from Cincinnati—or I did, a long time ago." He asked her who her acquaintance was. She gave him Joe's name and told him he had taught at Princeton High School, but she was reluctant to give the stranger her own full name. "Just tell him Barbara said hello." The visitor said he worked at General Electric near Princeton High School, and would try to find her old friend.

Some time went by and then the telephone call came. It was the young teacher—now twenty years older. He had never married. The tourist—we'll now call him Dudley and if you want to know why, just watch "The Bishop's Wife"—had found him, had come over from GE on his lunch hour to pass Barbara's message. But it took awhile for Joe to find Barbara because he didn't know her married name. After a period of fruit-less searching through a number of channels, Joe had finally remembered the name of a friend of Barbara and so had found her.

Having at last made the connection, Joe said, "Why don't you come over and see me, right now?" Barbara did and he asked her to marry him. (Incidentally, when she flew into the United States she landed in Florida, having no idea how far away Cincinnati was. Someone said that Americans think a hundred years is a long time, the English think a hundred miles is a long way.) Barbara was dumbfounded at receiving the proposal, but she decided yes and she and Joe were married.

The happy couple had Dudley's name and they went to GE to find him and to tell him their good news and how grateful they were. GE had no records of such a person. They never found the stranger, and Barbara says, "I still get goosebumps talking about it."

Remember to show hospitality. There are some who, by doing so, have entertained angels without knowing it (Hebrews 13:2).

Sara Sings and Sings

In a couple of weeks I will gather with others to bless Sara Holroyd's new, enlarged pond and waterfall, the latest addition to the small wonderland that is her back yard. Among the attractions are many kinds and great numbers of flowers, busy bird feeders, a fake frog that croaks as you walk by, and, my great delight, a G-gauge electric train with appropriate buildings and landscaping.

When Becky and I married a dozen years ago, the dowry was a passel of new people in my life. Sara was one of them. She had taught Becky in the music department of the university, and they had become friends. Over the years our relationship has become more nearly like family.

Mid-morning on most Saturdays Sara taps on our back door—lightly, in case anyone is still sleeping. She has been to the farmers' market early and brings flowers or vegetables and maybe some special bread or sweet pastry. We put the flowers in water, Becky makes coffee, and we settle in for an hour's talk. Mostly, I listen; the two women's minds are quick and the resulting conversation is faster than my ability to process. The Saturday morning visits are a comfortable time, a ritual we treasure.

Sara grew up in Alabama. She is in her early seventies, strong and vigorous, fascinated with life and deeply involved in it. She might have been a character in "Steel Magnolias." At sixty-two Sara took early retirement from her position as director of choral music at the university to start a new career. She went back to school and became a registered nurse. When her classmates chose her as valedictorian, Sara, a gifted soprano, sang her address.

Working in the emergency room of one of our city's busiest hospitals, she put her musical abilities to good use. Once an aged man had been brought in from the mountains; he was terrified and as Sara tended him she began to sing old, familiar hymns. As he listened he quieted. Not only was the old man affected; for a few minutes the whole atmosphere of the ER was transformed as the medical teams listened to music that, perhaps, took them back to another time and place and reminded them of why they were doing works of mercy.

Sara sings at church and with a group called the Sine Nomine Singers. She is often a soloist. Not long ago on a Sine Nomine program she had a solo part in one presentation. She sang from a score. When she had sung her way trough the first sheet she confidently turned to the second. Nightmare! It wasn't there. Sara knew the music, but not the words. So she improvised some words as she sang. They fit well enough and only her fellow musicians knew.

"O come, let us sing unto the Lord; let us heartily rejoice in the strength of our salvation. Let us come before his presence with thanksgiving, and show ourselves glad in him with psalms."

So begins the Venite, and the call to sing praise to God runs throughout the psalms, throughout the Bible. God's people are singers. The burial office's commendation contains these words: "All we go down to the dust; yet even at the grave we make our song: Alleluia, alleluia, alleluia." Every life sings some kind of song, and sometimes it's wonderful and sometimes it's off-key; sometimes we have the words, and sometimes we go "da, da, da, something, something."

God sings a song, and the song is life, us, all that lives, all that is. God intends our soul's song to be in harmony with his song.

Jesus taught, though not in so many words, that when we listen God teaches us his song—music and words. No improvisation necessary.

Angels All Around

Angels are "in" right now—books about meetings with angels; a *Time* magazine cover article—and before they go "out" again I have stories to tell. I'll tell four, but I have others.

A few weeks ago a mother who is a friend of my daughter was at a park with her six-year-old son. He asked to use a pitching machine to sharpen up his batting eye. What the mother didn't know was that the machine fired balls at 65 miles an hour. The boy missed the first pitch, changed his stance, and took the second one square in the chest. He went down and when his mother reached him he wasn't breathing and had no pulse.

Fortunately a nurse was nearby and came to help. By the time paramedics arrived the child was conscious and apparently okay. That night he told his parents (this is not an especially "religious" family, by the way), "While I was out I had a funny dream." "What was it?" they asked. "Oh, you wouldn't understand." "Try us." "Well, I dreamed I was in heaven and there were angels all around me."

Second story: I have a friend who is not given to flights of fancy. As a matter of fact she is one of the plainest talking, straight-shooting, meat-and-potatoes Christians I know. In a time of distress she distinctly heard a voice—during a football game, no less—tell her to read Revelation 2:10. She did and it helped. A short time later she received in the mail a bookmark, autographed by

Archbishop Ramsey. On the bookmark, sent by a friend hundreds of miles away and ignorant of the incident at the football game, was the passage from Revelation.

Third story: A friend—same sort of person—was driving with her daughter at night toward Lexington. They were in the right-hand lane of I-75. Up ahead a flashing arrow signaled for them to move to the left lane. My friend tried to turn the steering wheel. It wouldn't move. Then as the lane ended she tried desperately. The wheel still wouldn't turn . . . until a tractor trailer in the left lane, which had been riding in her blind spot, roared past. Then the steering wheel was released and at the last possible second the car moved into the left lane. My friend still keeps a little piece of chrome the truck chipped from her car.

Fourth story: I talked with Walt Johnson a few years after this happened. Some of the story is in his own words. Walt was editor of the *Middlesboro Daily News* in Kentucky. He was preparing to go fishing when his small daughter rushed into his house in nearby Cumberland Gap, Tennessee, saying the town was burning. He grabbed his camera. Some above-ground storage tanks at a service station had caught fire. He shot a number of pictures and then with a friend walked along a creek to within 100 yards of the station. He had been told the tanks had already exploded.

They hadn't and as he realized they were about to go Walt shouted a warning and his friend made it to safety beneath a railroad trestle. Walt ran but "it seemed only seconds until a monstrous concussion shook the earth and I was engulfed in yellow heat. Everywhere there was yellow heat, the mountain scenery was gone, the road was gone, Gap Creek was gone, it was all yellow burning heat.

"Making a dive for the creek, I came up short, floundering in foot-high grass. I tried to pull myself into the cold mountain stream, but couldn't find it. In irrationality, I cursed my friend for leading me to that side of the fire. Then it occurred to me that I was burning to death."

Walt prayed and "In the road which bent to my left was a tall grey figure standing calm and whose head was bent as if looking toward me. As suddenly as he had appeared, I felt a shock of peace, no burning, no pain. Without saying a word the figure communicated a feeling that I had an option to remain at peace in a restful death or to live." Walt thought, "I want to live."

At once he was on his feet and walking out of the fire, his clothes ablaze. His friend who had escaped put out the fire and got him to the hospital. Walt was terribly burned, but he lived.

Coincidence, dreams, hallucinations? Angels, I think. There is much more going on around us than we ordinarily see. Once in the days of the prophet Elisha the Arameans sent a large force to surround the town of Dothan. As dawn came Elisha's servant saw the Aramean army and exclaimed, "Oh, my lord! What are we to do?" Elisha said, "Have no fear; there are more on our side than on theirs," and he prayed and God opened the servant's eyes to see the mountain covered with horses and chariots of fire.

C.S. Lewis wrote in his space trilogy that to us an angel is a thin, half-real something that can go through walls and such, but in reality the angel goes through them because he is more solid and to the angel a wall or rock is like a cloud and "what is true light to him and fills the heaven, so that he will plunge into the rays of the sun to refresh himself from it, is to us the black nothing in the sky at night. These things are not strange . . . though they are beyond our senses."

Almost Home

Who said we are most ourselves when we are at home? Is that true? Who are we when we are at home?

Home is where the heart is. I think that's true. And I am reminded of an old prayer that asks God to send us to those whose "hearts are without a home." Our Book of Common Prayer speaks in one place of "this fragile earth, our island home." That's for now. But heaven is our true and final home. In our temporary home we sometimes think and act as if we were more important than other people, and in this world we may get by with that, but in the world to come it simply can't be. In the presence of God we are who we are, all equal, and we can't be anything else. It's a good idea to practice living that way while we are on the way home.

A little story:

Before I became a priest I was a newspaper reporter. For some of those years I was a member of my city's press club along with other newspaper, radio, and TV people, and a scattering of press secretaries and public relations people. It was great fun and I made some friendships in the press club that continue, more than 30 years later.

One of those friends is Glenn Kerfoot, who before his retirement was a writer for IBM. Glenn looks like a wrestler, and, except for the fact that his grammar and syntax are fine, sounds like one. He is a brilliant man with a wonderful sense of humor. For years he carried on a correspondence with the local newspaper letter column using the pseudonym "Professor Sigfried Haas."

Somewhere I have the professor's collected letters.

A favorite ploy, when he didn't want to talk on the phone (before the widespread use of the answering machine) was to answer it and say in a practiced oriental voice that this was "Missa Kerfoot's houseboy, Missa Kerfoot not home."

One night the press club was having a big party. I was emcee and was asking people to introduce themselves and their guests. When it came Glenn's turn he stood and said he would like us to greet his guest, Alan Paton, the South African author whose books were enjoying considerable celebrity at the time.

Well, as you can imagine, it created a sensation. In a minute we were all pushing and shoving to get near his table, lying about reading his books, fawning, and generally making fools of ourselves. You can probably guess the end of the story. The next day we learned that man wasn't Alan Paton, and we all laughed at Glenn's joke—a little uneasily, somewhat embarrassed.

That was pride, our pretending to be who we are not to impress Alan Paton. Far more dangerously, sometimes we do it to impress ourselves. Like mentally ill people who think so little of themselves that they invent stories or even believe themselves to be somebody else, somebody "more important."

Who are we when we are at home?

It's good to honor a person for a job well done, a life well lived. We can appreciate accomplishment, and God does too. Alan Paton, a Christian layman, wrote books that opened the eyes not only of people in South Africa, but throughout the world to the sin of oppression of other races, other peoples—*Cry the Beloved Country; Too Late the Phalarope*. But the hidden lesson in this story is that the man who pretended to be Alan Paton was important himself; not because of his assumed persona, but because he too was a dearly loved child of God.

It is wise never to think higher of ourselves than we ought and never to think lower of anybody else. At the same time we should never think lower of ourselves than we ought, because no matter what our social or economic status, we are equally as precious to God as the president, Mother Teresa, Queen Elizabeth, or Alan Paton.

Certainly the good we do is pleasing to God, but God doesn't love us more or less because of our fame or status. God loves the janitor in the sub-basement of the UN building as much as he loves the secretary-general, and the struggling single mother in a housing project as much as the governor of the commonwealth; and God loves the Iraqi gunners as much as he loves the American airmen who bomb them.

Who are we when we are at home? When we concern ourselves with being at home we realize that we are all the much-loved children of God, and we rejoice in that love, which is lavished not only on us but on every human being on the planet, in every age.

If for one day—one day—we could get this truth across to the people of the world, we would lay down our weapons and our pretenses, and fall into each other's arms weeping and begging forgiveness. And then we would sit down together and eat and drink and laugh, rejoicing in who you are and who I am and who our Father is.

Then we would be almost home, almost home.

Going 'Up Top'

In 25 years of priesthood I have served for shorter or longer periods in eight churches of the Diocese of Lexington, from the biggest to the almost smallest. I have learned from all of them, but there is something special, a depth of association, in my memories of the smaller churches.

The rootedness of generations, the long continuing relationships of individuals and families, their common histories, their shared experience of joy and sorrow, triumph and failure, birth and death, their traditions, their devotion to family and community, their hand-to-hand struggles of goodness and evil—in all this I see a richness of character, a definition of personality, a sharper image of human reality, that is missing in our larger society. I have learned something in these communities that I draw upon to keep in touch with humanity—including my own—who we are, who we were, who we might be. For the rest of my life I will remember and draw upon the remembrance of my time among the people of such places as St. Stephen's, Latonia; the Church of the Advent, Cynthiana; and St. Thomas, Beattyville. From them I have many stories that might begin, "The Kingdom of God is something like this . . ."

For a little more than three years I was supply priest for St. Thomas. Not long before I left, Anna Sherrow, one of the older members, died, and the funeral was set for a Sunday afternoon.

Just after lunch I went down the hill from the church

to the Newnam Funeral Home and made my preparations. While I was waiting to begin the service I sat in the office looking out the window. I noticed an old man dressed in jeans, work shirt, and straw hat—a summer uniform familiar to us middle-Americans. He either sat on the bench outside or walked about in its vicinity. I didn't recognize him and I didn't see him in the chapel during the service.

The burial was to be in the Proctor Cemetery. Proctor is a little community on a hill on the other side of the Kentucky River. My car was to follow right behind the funeral director's. Mr. Newnam had driven away and was blocking traffic on the main street. I was about to pull out of the parking lot when someone tapped on the driver-side window.

It was the old man. He said he wanted to go "up top." I said I was going to the Proctor Cemetery if he wanted a ride. He said he wanted to go "up top." I repeated my offer.

Traffic was backing up on the main street and Mr. Newnam was emerging from his car to see what the holdup was. At last the old man quit our conversation and got in the car. As we drove through the town and across the bridge and started up the hill toward Proctor, it turned out he wasn't going to the burial; he just wanted a ride to visit some folk at Proctor.

As we turned off the highway he looked ahead and first said it didn't look as if his friends were home, then said, yes they were and would I stop right over there.

I didn't have a choice. I stopped to let him out and watched sadly as the lead car disappeared over a hill. I had never been to the Proctor Cemetery.

Fortunately, Mr. Newnam, understanding the situation, had slowed down and I and the rest of the funeral procession arrived shortly at the cemetery. I asked Mr. Newnam who the old man was. He smiled and said he was "Jockey" Combs, real name Albert. He was 92 years old, and when he wanted to get from one place to another he just asked for a ride and people gave it to him.

That was what struck me. When Mr. Combs needed a ride he asked for it and got it. He expected it to be given and the givers expected to give it. It was just the way they were. I think the Kingdom of Heaven is something like that.

When I stopped to let Mr. Combs out of my car, he opened the door, offered me his hand, and said, "If I never see you again in this world, I'll see you in heaven." Somehow, at the time, I felt he knew more about it than I did.

We shook on it.

Lunch with Lex

Fifty-five years after his mother's death, Stegner wrote to her about what it felt like to turn 80. "Instead of being embittered, or stoical, or calm, or resigned, or any of the standard things that a long life might have made me, I confess that I am often simply lost, as much in need of comfort, understanding, forgiveness, uncritical love—the things you used to give me—as I ever was at five, or ten, or fifteen."

I thought that wasn't a bad definition of the new commandment Jesus gave his disciples, to "love one another as I have loved you."

Take a walk with me in my hometown of Lexington. We'll go west on Main Street past Rupp Arena, where 25,000 people can be stored for a couple of hours during a basketball game, past Mary Todd Lincoln's home, where considerable history is stored, over the West Main Street Viaduct to two big cemeteries. We'll stop here for a few minutes.

On the left side of the street is Calvary Cemetery for Roman Catholics. On the right side is the Lexington Cemetery for everybody else—Jews, Muslims, agnostics, protestants. In the past there was also separation by race. Episcopalians have their own cemetery, but it's filled up.

When I was a kid there was a story about a ghost who walked each night between the two Main Street cemeteries, a protestant seeking his or her Roman Catholic love, or vice versa. People used to park along the street to watch for the ghost and claimed they saw it.

No one talks about it anymore. Either they've forgotten or the ghost finally gave it up or modern street lights have taken the fun out of ghost watching.

A look at one grave before we go. A great slab of stone engraved "King Solomon." William "King" Solomon was what in the early 1800s was called a bum. Although he was well liked and did odd jobs, he was overly fond of whiskey and kept getting arrested. Finally a judge sentenced him to nine months as an indentured servant—a slave—and he was bought by a friend, a free black woman known as Aunt Charlotte. He was white. She kept him out of trouble.

King Solomon became a hero during the cholera epidemic of 1833. Hundreds became ill and died—including Aunt Charlotte—and no one would handle the bodies and bury them except King Solomon. Afterward, no one complained about his drinking habits or his appearance.

From the cemeteries where we store our dead awaiting the resurrection we cross another viaduct. If you look out from the crest of this one, in all directions you see huge buildings, also used for storage, mostly of tobacco. I've heard that the one stretching north beside the railroad is supposed to be about a mile long. Lots of storage.

On the other side of the viaduct we come to a neighborhood called Meadowthorpe. There used to be a little airfield with a grass runway. Lindberg landed here once. Now there's a strip of shops and behind them an aging subdivision. On the other side of the street are more shops and behind them a stockyard and more storage buildings all the way to Irishtown and the old James E. Pepper Distillery where bourbon once was stored in charred barrels.

We stop at the Meadowthorpe Café, open from 6 a.m. to 9 p.m. Monday through Saturday. Home-cooked food, heavy, delicious food for people who work hard. I've known the proprietor for going on 40 years, since he had a beanery downtown across from city hall when I was a reporter. (Once I noticed a sign in the window, "Restaurant for sale." As I paid my bill, I asked the old man about it. He laughed and said it's been for sale for 20 years and he'll sell when he gets the right offer. I don't think he really wants one.)

Now, further west toward more storage, this time for people: the federal prison and the huge VA hospital. It's to the hospital I've been leading you, where they keep veterans who are disabled and have nowhere else to go. This is where my friend Lex lived. Lex had a long contest with the government about his disability. He and a VA psychiatrist claimed he was disabled during service in the Navy. The VA said the psychiatrist's report came too late and didn't constitute new evidence, although she was a VA doctor. Lex's only option was to take his case to the VA appeals court in Washington. The VA limits to $10.00 the fee a lawyer can charge to represent a veteran making an appeal. Not enough for a D.C. lunch or a moderate-length long-distance call.

So Lex lived at the hospital and made the best of it. Although he had had a stroke a few years ago and had a problem talking and controlling arm and leg movements, he painted, and a few of his paintings hang in galleries and some have sold. I have a few.

After the Navy and before his troubles started, Lex went for a year to Purdue, where he was a whiz at math. A few years ago, after his stroke and with a tutor's help, he finally received his bachelor's degree from Brescia College, *cum laude*. He was a very smart man and I was challenged in our conversations.

Lex had lots of time to think, and he thought about God. He asked me a lot of questions and we had debates on points of theology. Some days Lex accepted what he considered the supernatural tenets of Christianity; other days he had some doubts. On all days he believed in God and believed that God is love and that human beings are here to love each other.

Lex lived in an environment in which the attendants were often detached from the patients, and the patients had little interest in each other, passing their days watching TV, waiting for meals, going outside for a smoke. Lex had a smile and an offer of conversation—or maybe a precious cigarette—for anyone who was interested, despite the fact that they could understand only a little of what he said. He had a bit of money some time back, but he gave most of it away. Lex genuinely loved life and other people.

Lex was very tall, very big, walked with a stumbling gait, and spoke unclearly. People sometimes found his appearance intimidating. Once workers in a general hospital cafeteria called for security believing he was drunk. He was embarrassed and hurt, even though he understood their mistake. Another day he spoke to a child on the street and a policeman stopped him for questioning.

"Love one another as I have loved you." Lex found it a little scary to be a demonstratively loving person out in the world, knowing some people would reject him, and the police might arrest him. That happened, too. Still, he kept trying.

Lex tried to love as Jesus loved—in the face of rejection and the threat of something worse. He was, in a way, a living reminder both of how we Christians are supposed to love and how, in practice, we do love—tentatively, stumblingly, not always clear in our expression, sometimes fearful. And yet most of us grit our teeth and after failure, try again. Not yet perfect in our belief, not yet perfect in loving others as Jesus loves us, we go on. Like Lex, even on our off days we are pretty sure that there is a God and that if God is anything God is love.

Lex and I used to go to lunch almost every week, sometimes at the Meadowthorpe Cafe—beans and cornbread, meatloaf with mashed potatoes and gravy—and we talked about this and that, and always about God and love.

Because of his speech problems I probably didn't catch more than half of what he said, and because I often have a weak voice and he had impaired hearing I suspect he didn't catch half of what I said. Still, as we spent time together at the table, we both learned a little more and then a little more about God's love and Jesus' love and how we loved ones should love each other.

David, Hattie, and Dogs

David was the meanest person on our block and Hattie the craziest. At least that's the way I saw it when I was a kid.

Our extended family lived in a rambling old house my grandfather had bought in the mid-thirties. The neighborhood was a wonderful mix of well-to-do and Depression-poor families. For the most part, the grander houses were occupied by widows of merchants; many of the less-than-grand had been divided into apartments.

And there were teachers. The principal and two teachers from my junior high school lived there. If I took a "sick day" I didn't dare go out of the house after school let out.

David and Hattie weren't our only characters. For instance, when lightning struck iron work at the top of the biggest house on the street, setting fire to its tower, the blast of thunder brought a crowd who watched firemen extinguish the modest blaze. At some point near the end of the scene the lady of the house opened a third-floor window and asked politely, "Am I on fire?"

David and Hattie were the two characters I knew best. He was our next door neighbor. Our houses were close together and in warm weather no one had secrets. When I was very small David complained that I made too much noise playing in our back yard. My parents gave him an earful. After that his biggest and most abiding complaint was about my uncle's two dogs, who were friendly but enjoyed barking. Occasionally David made overtures to the dogs, but they knew he was faking it and after taking his treats were as vocal as ever.

Hattie lived three houses away from us—four from David. I called her the dog woman until my parents found out and made me stop. I didn't mean any disrespect, it was just the observation of a little kid. She believed dogs were reincarnated people and kindly took in every stray that came along, and there were a lot of them in that time before strict animal control laws and routine neutering. Dog after dog after dog, and Hattie lived in a modest-sized bungalow with virtually no yard. The dogs lived inside. No one knew how many there were. On the few occasions when we visited her, there were always several dogs in the living room, and we could only guess how many lived in other parts of the house. Hattie took good care of the dogs, and her house was clean. But dogs do smell, and many dogs smell mightily.

Once neighbors two doors further on from Hattie's house filed a complaint about the smell. Actually, there was no smell outside her house. It was just that the people, among the last well-to-do residents, didn't appreciate Hattie's dog hostel. Hattie was to appear in magistrate's court and asked my mother to come as a witness for her. Mom, knowing how I liked to tell everything I knew, cautioned me not to say anything to David. I was standing on the sidewalk, dressed up for court when David came by and asked where I was going. I told him.

My mother was furious. David showed up in court to support the claim of pervasive dog smell, but since we lived nearer Hattie's house and my mother said there was no smell, the magistrate dismissed the case. David was furious.

A few years later—is this irony?—it was David who first noticed that Hattie's house was on fire. Instead of going directly to her, David told my father and my father told Hattie. We didn't get an accurate count of the dogs that day, but the number was beyond our imaginings. Hattie carried out dogs and put them in her car. She carried out dogs and put them in our front hall. Then she carried out dogs and put them in other cars parked along the street. I don't know where else they were stowed. It was, for us kids, a day of great excitement: first a fire and then all those dogs. No one, regular or reincarnated, was hurt.

David was still complaining about my uncle's dogs when my parents and I moved away. I never met him after that, but many years later when I was in the neighborhood I saw him occasionally, now an old man, living alone—except for, of all things, the dog he took for walks along Broadway.

If you look carefully, there is in this story something about not judging others, being good neighbors, reform, redemption, and maybe the paradox of bad theology (reincarnation) and good-heartedness (caring for strays).

All this came to mind one night after a friend stopped by with a puppy who needed a home. There were four tired people in our house when the puppy arrived, one or two a little grumpy. But a few minutes of puppy tail wagging and a happy puppy lick or two changed the mood.

The companionship of a dog tends to evoke our humanity. Which is what God intended all along. A transfiguration. We pray, we hope, that we are being transfigured into Christlikeness. Usually the change takes place gradually, and little by little we grow in grace and glow—if ever so dimly—with the glory of God.

We must be patient with each other and with ourselves until, as the prayer from Confirmation says it, being defended by God's grace, living as his children, daily increasing in his Holy Spirit, we come at last to his everlasting kingdom.

A Letter to Andrew

Andrew was born with an incomplete heart. When he was a little boy he wanted to play football; an extraordinary operation made it possible for him to do so. And to play baseball, basketball, and golf.

He was one of the children of my parish, St. Michael's, who asked questions that set me pondering the nature and the mystery of the Kingdom of Heaven. When Andrew died at age eighteen his parents brought out, to show the hundreds of mourners, photos and other treasures from their son's short and happy life. One item was a letter I had written Andrew when he was ten years old. (When the questions were hard I used my weak voice as an excuse to answer in writing, gaining time.)

The letter, dated February 27, 1985:

Dear Andrew,

You and I have never got around to talking about your question, "Why are we born?" and I want to say some things before I leave St. Michael's.

First of all, I don't think you were asking about how babies grow from an act of love between mother and father and how they're physically born in the world. If you don't know about that, your mother and father can help you understand.

"Why" is a very big word, and it's one of the things that separates us from the other animals. Science keeps telling us more and more about "how" things happen, but "why" remains a question always. You might say that "why" is the question of mankind. No matter how

much we learn, there is always something mysterious about life, about birth and death, about love and fear, about good and evil.

I'll tell you what I believe, and I believe it because of what I read about Jesus—say in the Gospel of St. John—and because when I trusted in what Jesus said and did, I found it was true. (That's a confusing sentence. Let me see if I can say it plainer.) Jesus showed us that God is like a loving father. When we respond to his love by loving him and each other, life is good, even when it's hard. I believe we're born because God is a lover and when a baby is born into the world it's another opportunity for him to love someone. And even before that I believe God loves us into being through our parents' love for each other. In the Confirmation class last week, one of the children said, "God is love—and nothing else."

This has been a long answer. I hope it wasn't confusing. The short answer may just be what the child said, "God is love—and nothing else."